D1374004

4-16-70

The Burial of Count Orgaz, by El Greco (1541–1614)
Church of Saint Thomas, Toledo, Spain
(Anderson—Art Reference Bureau)

JOHN DONNE'S CHRISTIAN VOCATION

Robert S. Jackson

1970

NORTHWESTERN

UNIVERSITY PRESS

EVANSTON

Robert S. Jackson is Associate Professor of English
at Rockford College, Rockford, Illinois

Permission to use material included in this book has been granted
by the following: The Clarendon Press, Oxford, for quotations
from Helen Gardner's *John Donne: The Divine Poems* (1952),
Herbert J. C. Grierson's *The Poems of John Donne,* Vol. I
(1912), and Evelyn M. Simpson's *A Study of the Prose Works
of John Donne* (2d ed., 1948); Dodd, Mead & Co. for quota-
tions from Edmund Gosse's *The Life and Letters of John Donne*
(1899); Evelyn Hardy for a quotation from her *Donne: A Spirit
in Conflict* (1942); The Johns Hopkins Press for quotations
from Frank Manley's *John Donne: The Anniversaries* (1963);
The National Council of Churches of Christ in the U.S.A. for
quotations from the *Revised Standard Version Bible;* Thomas
Nelson & Sons Ltd. for quotations from *Izaak Walton's Lives*
(n.d.); A. R. Mowbray & Co. Ltd. for quotations from W. H.
Longridge's translation of *The Spiritual Exercises of Saint
Ignatius of Loyola* (5th ed., 1955); and Random House, Inc.,
for quotations from Anton C. Pegis' edition of the *Basic Writings
of Saint Thomas Aquinas,* Vol. II (copyright 1945).

1546483

FOR
CHAD WALSH

CONTENTS

Frontispiece

Acknowledgments   *vii*

I   INTRODUCTION: *The World Movement of Donne's Lifetime*   *3*

II   THE BEGINNINGS OF TROUBLE: *Inner and Outer*   22

III   MANNERISM   39

IV   "RESOLUTION" DECLINED   56

V   THE DEPTHS   80

VI   THE PSYCHIC MARRIAGE   98

VII   CHURCH AND STATE   *123*

VIII   DONNE'S SONNET ON CHRIST'S SPOUSE   *146*

Appendix   *179*

Index   *181*

ACKNOWLEDGMENTS

All of the important assistance I have received over the years in developing the background for writing this book is too varied to acknowledge in detail. It will have to suffice to mention simply my parents and many professional and nonprofessional associates, particularly at Beloit College, the University of Michigan English department, Harvard Divinity School, Yale Divinity School and Yale College, and Kent State University. I should like to mention, in this general way also, many priests and clergy, particularly of the Anglican communion, but including, too, many persons of the religious brotherhood in its widest and deepest forms. I give a special thanks to the many graduate and undergraduate students at Kent State University who have lived through with me in my classes the developing stages of many of the matters presented in this book.

Some persons I would like to name. Aubrey Hastings, O. William and Eila Perlmutter, Frank Manley, Stanley Leavy, Jerome and Beverley Enright, Philip and Cordelia Koplow, and Daniel Brewer have read portions of the manuscript and provided sustaining encouragement. The same has been done by Louis Martz, Martin Havran, Joseph Politella, Robert Tener, and Kenneth Pringle, who have also added helpful suggestions. Jacob Leed has read the entire manuscript twice, except one late chapter, and has been of inestimable help in understanding me and it during its various stages of growth. Chad Walsh has helped with the manuscript, and as a teacher and friend for twenty-three years has given me other assistances too numerous to mention; to him I dedicate the book. My wife, Jacqueline, has not only lived through the difficulties occasioned by the writing of this book but has also given her expert editorial guidance over most of its chapters. Anne Reid has provided some editorial as well as secretarial help. To each of these persons I give my thanks.

I would like to express here my appreciation also to the Gestalt Institute in Cleveland, Ohio, for sponsoring a workshop in 1964–65 through which Ira Progoff introduced me to Jungian thought; to the Northwestern University Press for their act of faith in publishing this book and in providing the assistance of Virginia Seidman for the exacting task of copyediting; to the Research Committee of Kent State University for the financial help of three separate grants; to the library staffs at Kent State University, the University of Vermont, St. Michael's College in Winooski, Vermont, Rockford College, the Houghton Library, the Newberry Library; and to Rockford College for secretarial and duplicating assistance.

ROBERT S. JACKSON

Rockford College
Rockford, Illinois
January, 1970

JOHN DONNE'S
CHRISTIAN VOCATION

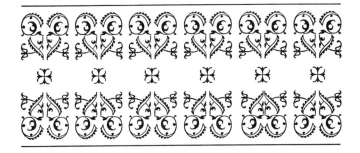

CHAPTER I

INTRODUCTION:
The World Movement of Donne's Lifetime

When I began to study Donne's *Devotions* several years ago, I found that I had to try to understand the man John Donne and his world, particularly the religious climate, before I could find the terms in which to say something genuinely meaningful about the work. I knew from reading Louis Martz's *Poetry of Meditation*[1] and from my own work on the Ignatian background of Jeremy Taylor's *The Great Exemplar*[2] that Donne's *Devotions* represented a somewhat Calvinized version of the tradition of Loyola's *Spiritual Exercises:* Donne there contemplates

---

1. Louis Martz, *The Poetry of Meditation: A Study in English Religious Literature of the Seventeenth Century* (New Haven: Yale University Press, 1954).

2. *The Meditative Life of Christ: A Study of the Background and Structure of Jeremy Taylor's "The Great Exemplar,"* Ph.D. diss., University of Michigan, 1958 (Ann Arbor: University Microfilms, 1959).

depraved man—his own sick body—rather than the glorified person of the archetypally whole man, Jesus, as the *Spiritual Exercises* had done. But to state it that way as a mere academic disclosure—this and this are true facts—did not seem to be enough. What did that have to do with man's actual existence, Donne's existence, mine, the existence of other men, both then and now? Donne's book had a reality and a depth that connected it to the great issues of life and death, which are our issues as well as his. If I were really to read the *Devotions,* I had somehow to enter the kinds of reality which they expressed. I searched into Donne's life and background to see if I could understand what actually had gone into their making, and I searched both objectively and subjectively into my own life and culture to try to find the language which would make the results of that study communicable to the persons in my own time who might be interested—family, personal friends, graduate students, professional colleagues. In the process the *Devotions* were left behind and the present book emerged. It is an effort to recreate the movement of some fifteen or more years in Donne's lifetime during which he faced and resolved most of the difficulties standing between him and his vocation to the priesthood in the Anglican church.

Have I apprehended him in his terms? or our own? or my own? In all three ways, inescapably, it seems to me. More than three hundred years have passed since Donne died, and the commonplace way of speaking about that is to say that we live in another world. But, literally speaking, that is a falsehood. "His world" does not exist. There is only one world, and it is the world we live in. And that world is the same one in which he once lived, modified of course by the stresses and strains, the growth and decay, warpings and relocations, by which the processes of time do their work. The world moves and changes, but it does not vanish only to be replaced by another of nearly the same sort.

Like the world outside him, so does man himself move, so that, when he is born, changing man joins a world in motion. Coming into existence is more like running to jump on a moving train than like the placing of one fixed counter called "me" upon another fixed and defined territory called "the world." So it is for all of us, and so it was for John Donne, who was born into a world which, like our own, was rapidly moving out of its own past through the agency of a violently agitated present into an uncertain and only dimly apprehended future.

In order to gain any clarity at all about what this world is that we have come into and what we are to do in it, we must sometimes "stop" this action, as though by a photograph taken with a high-speed shutter. That is essentially what a book is, taken all together, and it is what this book is and what this chapter is. But whether the "photograph" be of a more remote or a more immediate past, and whether it be "stopped" by the apparent stasis of chemical emulsion or of printed words on a printed page, we may never rightly forget that the reality which the picture represents occurred as part of the world flow, the same basic world flow which we ourselves experience in our own lives in the world. In this sense, the act of reading, with its entry into a serial movement of language and internal events happening one after the other, is a better metaphor for the reality of the world experience than the totality of the finished product. Neither the world nor any book is ever finished. Both exist in process, regardless of our use of single nouns like "book" and "world," as though they were eternal objects. Persons like objects play a part in the world process, however small or great. So did John Donne, so will this book, and so indeed will John Donne partly through this book.

Though I make use of many kinds of scholarly methods to tell the story I have undertaken here, some more and some less conventional—historical, literary, critical, psychological, mythical, phenomenological—the book is fundamentally a biographical study. As such, it appears to stop the world movement at the stage in which its leading character played his role. And the peculiar configuration of any culture at a particular time in the past is often apprehended by us only with difficulty, so changed and reshaped has it become since then.

That is the kind of difficulty which causes many scholars to try to do what they call a strictly "historical" study, which means to describe their subject in the terms which its contemporaries used. This is the proper way to study "mannerism," for example, says John Shearman in his recent book on that subject: "In my view," he says, "the contradictions in contemporary meanings for the word 'Mannerism' are to a great extent due to the fact that most of them are too contemporary and not sufficiently historical." [3] In Shearman's eyes and the eyes of those like him, I shall be adding to the confusions and contradictions. By the term "mannerism" I refer to any style of disjunction between a pair of polar opposites where the way between the poles is invisible or, if visible, is vague, strained, twisted, or contorted.[4] It can refer to a disjunction between the polar

---

3. John Shearman, *Mannerism* (Harmondsworth, Eng.: Pelican Original, 1967), p. 15.
4. The term originated in art history. Heinrich Wöfflin's definitive *Principles of Art History* (trans. M. D. Hottinger, 7th ed. [New York: Dover Publications, n.d.]) compares a Renaissance with a Baroque style. Mannerism is usually said to occupy the space between this Renaissance and Baroque style and, until recently, has been often passed over as a transitional art form. Two important recent books which have attended more closely to this in-between period are Franzepp Würtenberger's *Mannerism: The European Style of the 16th Century*, trans. Michael Heron (New York: Weidenfeld & Nicholson, 1963), and Arnold Hauser's *Mannerism: The Crisis of the Renaissance and the*

aspects of a work of art, but it may also signify the mode of
relationship between a man and a work of art, or between a
man and the world, or between the polar aspects of a man;
hence, it can refer to a life style as well as an aesthetic style.
It can refer to a disjunction between two periods of time, as
between ourselves and John Donne. In a sense, therefore,
my own book is a mannerist book, since it expresses a
strained communication between myself and John Donne,
in which I adopt now a critical stance toward him and now
an uncritical one, now see him as though he were far off
from me and now as though he were nearly myself; and I
join those two positions dimly, by analogy or by intuition
rather than by logical or Scholastic methods.

I do not assume that Donne's only proper or intended
audience was his own contemporaries, as though reality
were only horizontal in space and that we, coming later in
time, are mere eavesdroppers. The reality of past time is in
our present; and when I say that, I am affirming an Augus-
tinian model of time, but I am not being antihistorical or
even ahistorical. I am interested in historical procedures,
but I am interested in them only insofar as they improve

Origin of Modern Art, trans. Eric Mosbacher, 2 vols. (New York:
A. A. Knopf, 1965). Hauser, for whom mannerism is a general
cultural term, specifically treats Donne as a mannerist, especially
in his chapters entitled "The Disintegration of the Renaissance,"
"Mannerism in Art and Literature," and "The Principal Repre-
sentatives of Mannerism in Western Literature." See also John
Shearman's book cited in the text and in n. 3, above. Wölfflin's
book first appeared in German in 1915 (first English trans. in
1932), Würtenberger's in 1962, and Hauser's in 1965. More
important for literary studies are Roy Daniells' *Milton, Man-
nerism and Baroque* (Toronto: University of Toronto Press,
1963), whose view, however, I have in part disputed in my
article "Michelangelo's Ricetto of the Laurentian Library: A
Phenomenology of the Alinari Photograph," *Art Journal,* XXVIII
(Fall, 1968), 54–58, and Wylie Sypher's *Four Stages of Renais-
sance Style* (New York: Doubleday, 1956). Donne is probably
the chief literary figure in Sypher's chapter on "Mannerism." On
my own use of the term see also Chapter III.

our own apprehension of Donne. Indeed, it seems to me that we come to John Donne with certain special accesses which were not available to his own contemporaries; we can all read "Show me deare Christ," for example. How many of his contemporaries could is not clear, but it could not have been many, since the poem has been preserved in a unique manuscript copy. Consequently, I make use of mannerism, for example, in the way most helpful for the special aspect of Donne's life which I am describing here. Nor do I avoid using Carl Jung to interpret Donne's archetypal experiences merely because Donne or his contemporaries would have used Plato or some other "historical" figure for the same purpose. Jung's "archetypes" are essentially the same as Plato's "ideas," but most modern students will make a research project out of Plato and that will falsify him; Donne's readers would not have done so. However, I make use of Carl Jung's concepts as I do of the concept of mannerism, not strictly as the originator used them but flexibly, supposing that Jung (and Plato too) had given them to me, freely and generously, for that purpose.

Those who cry "history" the loudest and most insistently are most antihistorical, since it is they who most of all disbelieve in its genuine existence. Their very motive for insisting on it so dogmatically is to isolate it from the present. In this way they destroy its reality as best they can, justifying that act in the name of truth, accuracy, and fact. Nowhere has this attitude prevailed more exclusively than when the subject matter is religious, since it is widely assumed among scholars that, even if other aspects of our inherited culture may continue to have some vitality, religious subject matter may not. For this area—or what is given this name, since it actually pervades all human existence in one mode or another—a special taboo prevails; it may be treated only as "history," and in no other way. Or rather, it may be treated as alive only within the exclusive confines of a cult group which we may not be permitted to believe has any continuity with the culture at large. I do not accept these taboos and dogmas, and I invite the reader, likewise, to shake them off. The first one infringes upon academic freedom, and the second one is a manifest falsehood. Religious language, symbols, values, and traditions certainly do have vitality outside the cult groups which protect or nurture them in a special way. For us to think otherwise is simply to close our eyes to our own culture. It is necessary to say this because it is John Donne's religious life, in the conventional sense of that term, which is the concern of this book. That means, of course, a certain kind of Christianity. It is upon this that I have concentrated, especially upon certain "spiritual" and biblical aspects of the Christian tradition, and I have handled these aspects freely in the terms in which they might be understood to have meaning now, in ways which for some people seem to be taboo.

Yet I do not wish to treat Donne's Christianity as an isolated phenomenon. It emerged and took shape as part of the total world experience, one aspect of which he lived through and contributed to. I call this world movement of Donne's lifetime by the Janus-headed term "Renaissance-Reformation," and I discuss it in this introductory chapter by the method of the phenomenology of history in order to set the metaphysical tone into which I would like the more particular study which follows to appear. I consider the method of phenomenology to be genuinely historical, although I am aware that for many scholars—especially those committed to a static view of the nature of the past—it will not be considered such. The phenomenological method requires that we acknowledge our own participation in the reality and the nature of the past by our own act of apprehending it. Although in studying a seventeenth-cen-

tury subject we may be jumping onto one of the rear cars
of the train of history—really a middle car, considering the
whole indefinite length of that train—it is we, now, in our
own reading experience, who are riding in that seven-
teenth-century car, at least for this small part of our jour-
ney.

I use the phrase Renaissance-Reformation to describe the
world of John Donne's lifetime in order to emphasize
certain relationships between these two terms which are
often ignored in their usual separated form. It is perfectly
appropriate that we should use a dual term to express that
historical period which succeeded the "medieval" because,
as all students of the later period know, the growth of a
sense of duality is one of its most distinguishing characteris-
tics. Yet, at the same time, it is fundamentally false to the
sense of those times to imagine that this duality is absolute.
Things appeared to them in twos, but in sets of twos which
in some way or another, often shadowy, belonged to part of
some wholeness. This can be apprehended as the wholeness
which survived from the earlier period or which *might*
belong to that wholeness if only they knew how to find it.
They had not yet surrendered to dichotomy or to fragmen-
tation. They felt themselves part of a world which was
growing more and more polarized but whose tensions and
apparent dichotomies could still be resolved, whether by
some more or less gradual and harmonious means, as had
tended to be characteristic of the Elizabethans (and in a
different way later on, in baroque art), or by some paradox-
ical or nearly miraculous intuitive leap, as was more charac-
teristic of Donne's experience and of the metaphysicals
generally.

The duality between past and present was one of the
most important felt during Donne's lifetime. It is familiar
to ourselves, as are, indeed, most of the other dualities
experienced during his time—and naturally enough, since

Donne's experience and agony represented the birth pangs
of modernity. Persons living in the power center of the
twin movement of the Reformation-Renaissance, as he did,
were made more and more aware of their own present as a
revolutionary time, a time to be set into sharp contrast with
the past through which history had just come. That imme-
diate past they now apprehended as the "Middle Ages," a
period intermediate between the origin or source of history
and their own present. That experience of duality in history
between the source and the present was not reduced,
whether the language about history was phrased in terms
of decadence, decay, death, and passing-away (which is the
aspect of the immediate past) or in terms of birth, newness,
and life (which is the aspect of the future coming-into-
being-now). It is partly because of the continuity of this
mode of apprehension that we do not ourselves make so
sharp a distinction between the medieval period and the
Reformation-Renaissance as they did. From our point of
view, much later in time, John Donne and his contempo-
raries lie almost as much in the intermediate period of
history as do Abelard and Heloïse. We distinguish between
our present and theirs just as they did between their present
and the medieval style they inherited and were busy trans-
forming and replacing.[5] The people of the late medieval
period had lived within and upon an immensely elaborated
hierarchy of discrete and separable levels or steps which
had functioned to join the fundamental duality of existence
whose paradigm is usually expressed as this world and the
other. These ladderlike structures could be found almost
everywhere. They were the nine orders of angels, the three

5. This contemporary awareness of a great divide between our
own present and a now dead past, but a divide in a much more
recent period in history than the so-called Renaissance, is very
powerfully expressed in C. S. Lewis' inauguration speech at Cam-
bridge, *De descriptione temporum* (Cambridge, Eng.: At the
University Press, 1955).

steps of the spiritual life, the fourfold systems of interpreting the Scriptures. Or, turning to the aesthetic realm, they were in the series of discrete levels or planes which made up the picture's space in the graphic art of the Renaissance, as Wölfflin has pointed out so powerfully (his term "Renaissance" being the equivalent of my "late medieval").[6] The "ladder" is illustrated in the paintings of the Limburg brothers, for example. And it can be seen in Dante's multi-leveled *Purgatorio,* or in his *terza rima* verse form, or in the levels of meaning in his metaphors. Our own use of the metaphor of "ladder" to refer to hierarchy emphasizes its deadness; some kind of personified metaphor—heart, hands, head—would refer better to it in its aspect as a living organism.

Though this organization of reality was alive for the people who lived it, by the time of the Reformation-Renaissance it was dying for more and more people. It had had a profuse and luxuriant growth, but by the time of its demise it had become so subtle and complex that only a small number of highly developed and sensitive persons rightly placed by the conditions of their birth and environment were able to join it, while for larger and larger numbers of persons it was becoming irrelevant. And human beings cannot remain alive without joining the world stream. Human need gave rise to a new movement, a new way for personal life to enter into the world process. This new movement, withdrawing from the complex model of the late Middle Ages, transferred the power previously there into its own, in some senses simpler, model. Impatient with the multiplicity of levels formerly mediating those extremes, whether they were conceived in spiritual, ecclesiastical, social, or aesthetic terms, they kicked over the ladder and sought some way to join the

6. Wölfflin, *Principles of Art History,* esp. Chap. II, "Plane and Recession."

extremes by outflanking the gap or leaping it. This new movement was the Reformation-Renaissance, and its model of meaning was fundamentally two-staged, showing only the levels of this world and the other.

Consider the so-called religious form of this movement. It was the reformers, of course, who overthrew the established hierarchies of medieval Christendom. How completely they did so depended, of course, upon how radical this or that person or group carried out the reform, but the over-all movement is clear enough. Between this life and the next, they removed purgatory. Between human and divine being, they removed the saints. Between the Jesus of past time and the body of Christ at any particular present moment, transubstantiation was removed. Between the holy family in heaven and the humble laboring man, they removed the pope. And, in more radical groups, not only was the mediate figure of the pope removed, but so were the archbishop, the bishop, and the priest, leaving only the minister to be the mediating figure between God and man; and among the most radical reformers, notably the Quakers, even he was removed. Subsequent history has shown, I think it is fair to say, that the Reformation-Renaissance felt uneasy about the church itself, retaining it to the degree that they did rather to symbolize the other world than as a mediating institution.

Or consider the character of the changes undertaken on the Renaissance side of the new movement. The new things in the world of learning were Ramism and Platonism, and they were the tools by which medieval Scholasticism was swept away. What a multiplicity of steps of inference, of objections and answers to objections, had to be taken into account in moving between premises and conclusion in the logic of the *Summa,* for example! In Ramism the whole great scheme of qualities, causes, conditions, substances, and accidents which had gradually transformed a medieval stu-

dent from youthful ignorance into mature knowledge was
unnecessary. All that vast learning could be replaced with a
simple two-staged logic that could be learned overnight
and that did not need to take into account any more of
Aristotle than the law of the excluded middle. Students
were so delighted by all this that Justus Lipsius warned
one: "Young man, listen to me: You will never be a great
man if you think that Ramus was a great man." [7] To
acquire the new learning meant the accession of Platonic
insight. One needed simply a reversal of direction: one was
no longer to look outward at the world—that was the
shadow of truth, not its reality; one was to look inward,
toward the source—this was to see the light in Plato's
famous allegory of the cave. When a man had done that,
he was released from slavery to the world of illusion and
saw the truth, at least insofar as he was able to bear the
brightness of it. There was light and there was dark; there
was truth and there was falsehood; there was reality and
there was illusion. Platonic man lived in the presence of
these alternatives.

These many polarities, not in themselves new in the
Reformation-Renaissance but newly singled out as twin
centers of attention by the persons of that period, have
been frequently remarked upon in studies of the late six-
teenth and early seventeenth centuries. The divide between
the sacred and secular which creates the contrast upon
which this present study is founded is one important mode
of that over-all situation. Cavalier and Puritan, church and
state, man and God, sin and salvation, the one and the
many, body and soul, art and nature, intellect and emotion,
are a few more of the well-known variants. Others of
somewhat different and perhaps less familiar type are the

7. Quoted on the title page of Walter J. Ong, S.J., *Ramus:
Method, and the Decay of Dialogue* (Cambridge, Mass.: Harvard
University Press, 1958).

pairs male and female, you and me, here and there, now and then, inner and outer, speaker and hearer. But the list can be extended indefinitely.

The duality of past and present was perhaps the most fundamental. The moderns of that present had suddenly, as they felt, rediscovered the ancients, both classical and biblical. Yet even slight acquaintance with the Middle Ages shows that it was not ignorant of the Bible or of Plato. The difference was in the mode of apprehension. The Bible was present to the daily life of the Middle Ages through liturgy, art, drama, literature; it infiltrated through the *Divine Comedy* and the "Cherry-Tree Carol." And Plato was the catalyst by which the Aristotelianism of Saint Thomas was joined to Christian faith. But this earlier "infused" mode of apprehension was no longer interesting to the Reformation-Renaissance. The persons leading the new movement wanted a new antiquity, and they found it by intuiting an antiquity polarized from their own present. The very remoteness of this new antiquity provided the sense of excitement and discovery that they wanted, and in its presence the mediate antiquity of their fathers and grandfathers fell rapidly out of sight, so rapidly, indeed, that it seemed not to have been there at all. The men who had preceded them had rendered in-between things more clearly, bringing into focus the gradients that connected this to that, showing how you got from here to there; while they themselves now, in emptying out this mediate realm, exposed more nakedly the polarities which lay at the two extremes. It was as though the men of Donne's time wore historical bifocals which permitted them to juxtapose antiquity with the world immediately about them, leaving everything in between missing or, at best, out of focus.

The Bible was just as truly a rediscovery of antiquity as classical learning was. To rediscover the Bible meant to the Protestants to rediscover the original source of things in its purity, before history had been corrupted by "man's smudge and . . . man's smell," as Gerard Manley Hopkins expressed the condition which the reformers were more likely to describe by saying they had been "disceaved by mens tradicions." [8] The medieval period was the end product of a great decline in world history, down into which their own lives could slip unless a great power and energy from the very source of life itself could lift them across that depth, joining them to whatever brought both themselves and the world they lived in into existence. To become connected with the Bible, across the divide of man's history, was to become reconnected with original purity and vitality, and it would give man the help he needed to shift over from participating in the deepening corruption of the times recently past into bringing about the new world to come. When that happened, one's own life participated in bringing the new world into being. Man had himself to be remade, reformed, his primal matter reinspirited, in order to play his proper role in the world transformation. Since the materials out of which he and the rest of the world were made were rapidly passing away, man had to be rescued before he perished utterly, and this required some kind of radical change—at the heart. This change could actually happen; it could be experienced; and, when it did, something new entered the world. Man needed only to receive into the perishing part of himself the primitive and generative potency which was latent in himself from his own original participation in Adam. The Adam story above all—the story of the Garden and of the Fall—made an imaginative appeal; it was the story of man's birth, of his genesis. In a more hidden way but more profoundly important for the new birth was the New Testament story with

8. "Myles Coverdale unto the Christian Reader," quoted from my article "The 'Inspired' Style of the English Bible," *Journal of Bible and Religion,* XXIX (January, 1961), 8.

its new genesis of man, his second birth, in the Jesus who as the second Adam restored the fallen man to his true original manhood. When that second birth happened, something new entered the world—a man who was really alive, who actually existed. The excitement of rediscovering the classics of Greece and Rome functioned in much the same way. It was like becoming a whole man again. The presence of the ancient classics in one's own world represented the discovery in oneself of one's own primal life. The humanists not only rediscovered the past; they rediscovered themselves, and that was why they were so excited about it. They did so, of course, in the same style that they rediscovered history, bifocally, by leapfrogging their own mediate selves. To have looked within and discovered there the source of truth! Wasn't that wonderful? And wasn't that what Plato's allegory of the cave told them to do? Know thyself. Turn away from the shadows in the cave. Seek the light within. That was what it was to be a man. Not that one was to stay forever gazing upon that light. Neither the biblical nor the Platonic story brought one to that conclusion. In Plato's story, the man who had experienced the light of reality was to return to the cave, bringing his knowledge with him, no matter how painful the darkness of that world of illusion or the scorn of his fellows. The function of this experience was to remake the shadows by the remembered light of reality. And the new humanists brought out of their antique symbols the same kind of world-transforming zeal which the Protestant biblicists did out of theirs.

So the duality of the period was not the same as Manichaean dualism or any other kind of absolute dualism. The "rediscovery of antiquity" contained a profound ambivalence; while antiquity was apparently apprehended as extraordinarily remote from their own present, it was also secretly within the present. To "turn back to the past" meant to join the past to the present, to make it a part of one's own life. To experience antiquity was to be reunified, and, by living that paradox, the Reformation-Renaissance brought into existence its own peculiar style of history.

The sweeping-away of medieval methods therefore did not mean that no means of mediating the poles now existed. It was an apparent, not a real, loss. The restructuring of medieval logic during Donne's lifetime into Renaissance paradox, for example, did not bring about irreconcilable opposition. Paradox merely means something which *seems* to show irreconcilable opposition; it is an *apparent* dilemma. The resolution of the paradox may be mysterious, but the fact is indisputable. Nor were the medieval modes entirely swept away. The connection of Scholastic logic to Donne's metaphysical wit is usually undefined, but it is not necessarily absent. Or, to choose another example, when the Quakers made a radical cleansing of the old ecclesiastical "means of grace," they did not thereby find that grace had no means. Or when Francis Bacon swept aside the cobwebs of Scholastic language, which had previously mediated nature to man's mind, he certainly did not claim that no way could be found by which man's mind could apprehend nature.

The decisive purpose of this new direct confrontation of polarities across an apparently empty middle was not to make unity impossible but to provide a new style of achieving it—a simpler style, one which was rapid and dramatic. If, in the Middle Ages, the mediate way had to be in clearly defined stages, rendered in full daylight like the details in Botticelli's *Birth of Venus,* now the way was to become obscure and mysterious. If before it had been steps to be climbed, now it was a gulf to be leaped. If before it had been multiple, now it was to be single. If before, gradual, now sudden. The mode of relationship was to be changed but not yet to be eliminated. That came later, in England by means of the Puritan wars. In political terms it came in England with the severing of Charles's head from his body in 1649. In religious terms it is a little harder to define a precise moment; perhaps it came with the Toleration Act of 1689, which firmly established sectarianism as the cultural mode of the future. In poetry it is even more difficult to set a moment. But it is clear enough that John Donne did not give up the effort to achieve one world. Although Donne's resolution by paradox is hidden from verbal daylight, as though not present, yet all sensitive readers intuit its presence. The veil which is drawn over the mediate realm in much of the style of the Reformation-Renaissance does not destroy what it hides. And the man who has made the journey behind the veil leaves some tracks which can be dimly seen, even by us much later in time and even if one of the tracks we see is mystery itself.

Before I begin the particular story of Donne's vocational adventure, it will be interesting to see where all the uncertainties with which he began will finally lead. Outwardly they lead from the Catholic polarity of his childhood to his ordination in the Anglican church, an Anglicanism which in some way is both Catholic and Protestant. The usual way to express the inner poles of the religious life is to talk about doubt and faith. But if the end result is to join the poles in some sense, we can scarcely expect a simple movement, like changing from doubt to faith, but rather the achievement of some kind of faith which includes doubt as part of its wholeness. And in his late poem, "To Christ," that is precisely what we find. This is the poem also printed under the title "A Hymne to God the Father," beginning with "Wilt thou forgive that sinne where I begunne," continuing with a series of questions representing the history of the sins of his life, and concluding with the familiar forecast of his last sin:

> I have a sinne of feare, that when I have spunne
> My last thred, I shall perish on the shore;
> Sweare by thy selfe, that at my death thy Sunne
> Shall shine as it shines now, and heretofore;
> And, having done that, Thou hast done,
> I have no more.[9]

It seems at first reading that he is afraid there is no afterlife, that he will "perish on the shore." The language implies a land and an embarkation point, but it does not necessarily imply that there is another shore and another land; and that in itself suggests the mystery and the doubt-fulness. The problem of death is the problem of facing the unknown. But insofar as it comes from the world of natural experience the figure also suggests an aspect of confidence. "The farther off from England, the nearer is to France," says the whiting in *Alice in Wonderland*. When you set out from the shore of England across the Channel, there is a land on the other side; and Donne had once experienced fear about perishing on that ordinary journey, as he shows in the "A Valediction: of weeping," as well as confi-dence, in that he actually did make the journey. Of course the earlier fear had been conditioned by his love for some-one left behind. But so is this later fear conditioned by love. It is indicated in the feeling for the shore, for the world itself; it is in the very writing of the poem—so that persons in the existing world can read it. It is also indicated by the demand that the "Sunne" shine then at his death as it has been shining before. In the "Sunne" metaphor the word standing for the natural experience is joined by the "Son," representing the more-than-natural, and by this means the two shores, or the two worlds, are joined. So doubt is

9. I have used the text appearing in Helen Gardner, *John Donne: The Divine Poems,* printed from corrected sheets of the first edition, 2d ed. (Oxford: Oxford University Press, 1964), p. 51.

expressed in the confession with which the stanza opens and faith in the demand of lines three and four, followed by the surrender of the last two lines. Is this a "religious" or a "secular" poem? By calling it religious we may succeed in isolating our own fears about death from John Donne's. We may think that only such a modern poem as Dylan Thomas' "Do not go gentle into that good night" can represent our experience—that the religious and the nonreligious cannot be joined. If so, we are victimized by our own presuppositions, and our power to receive what John Donne has to say is impoverished. We must be prepared to believe that the religious is not utterly "other" from the nonreligious before we can follow along the route that John Donne took. And if some reader think I have left out the essential meaning that should be found in the religious life, I reply that the element they ask for is not for me to supply: Donne says somewhere that he "would have no such readers as he could teach," a remark which C. S. Lewis holds against him as "dandyism." [10] Maybe so; but Lewis certainly should have known that the conventional religious word for it is "humility."

10. "Donne and Love Poetry in the Seventeenth Century," in William R. Keast, ed., *Seventeenth-Century English Poetry: Modern Essays in Criticism* (New York: Oxford University Press, Galaxy Books, 1962), p. 98; reprinted from *Seventeenth-Century Studies Presented to Sir Herbert Grierson* (Oxford: Oxford University Press, 1938).

CHAPTER II

THE BEGINNINGS
OF TROUBLE:
Outer and Inner

John Donne, Ann Donne, Un-done" goes the well-known epigram in which John Donne celebrated the consequences of his marriage, a marriage which Izaak Walton, in his mildly obtuse way, called "the remarkable error of his life." [1] A little younger than thirty at the time,[2] Donne had been secretary to Sir Thomas Egerton, then lord keeper (later lord high chancellor) of England. His pros-

---

1. "The Life of Dr. John Donne," *Izaak Walton's Lives,* The Nelson Classics (London: Thomas Nelson & Sons, n.d.), p. 51. This edition of Donne's life is Walton's final revision (1675).

2. I consider his birth date to be early in 1572, prior to June 19 of that year. In this I follow what seems to me to be the most probable date, based on the summary of evidence given by Evelyn M. Simpson in her chapter entitled "Sketch of Donne's Life" in *A Study of the Prose Works of John Donne,* 2d ed. (Oxford University Press, 1948), pp. 12–13. The rest of the biographical information here, and elsewhere in the book unless I have indicated to the contrary, is from Edmund Gosse, *The Life and Letters of John Donne: Dean of St. Paul's,* 2 vols. (New York: Dodd, Mead, 1899) (hereafter cited as Gosse, *Life*).

pects were good. But when he impulsively ran off and married Ann More without notifying her powerful and irascible father, Sir George More, the result was apparent disaster.

Having begun with this personal, romantic style of behavior and pushed it far enough to discover its effect, he then doubled back and pursued the more conservative style, hoping to gain the values of both. Thus, he first proved that he could separate the daughter from the father without following proper channels, and, after putting that separation beyond recall, he attempted to secure a traditional relationship with her father after all. Not quite up to facing Sir George in person, Donne notified him by letter, stating that he had acted well from his own point of view and that, since there was nothing his father-in-law could do about it, he had better forgive them and help his daughter and her husband in whatever way he could. In order to start the reader off with a sizable and authentic experience of Donne's own life and writing, I quote that letter in full. But what kind of letter shall we call it? An apology? or a demand? Charity would perhaps reconcile those two and call it an explanation. Its involuted syntax no doubt proceeds directly from the combined anxiety and boldness with which Donne makes his first belated approach to his father-in-law:

> SIR,—If a very respective fear of your displeasure, and a doubt that my lord [Sir Thomas Egerton] (whom I know, out of your worthiness, to love you much) would be so compassionate with you as to add his anger to yours, did not so much increase my sickness as that I cannot stir, I had taken the boldness to have done the office of this letter by waiting upon you myself to have given you truth and clearness of this matter between your daughter and me, and to show you plainly the limits of our fault, by which I know your wisdom will proportion the punishment.

So long since as her being at York House this had
foundation, and so much then of promise and contract built
upon it as, without violence to conscience, might not be
shaken.

At her lying in town this Parliament I found means to
see her twice or thrice. We both knew the obligations that
lay upon us, and we adventured equally; and about three
weeks before Christmas we married. And as at the doing
there were not used above five persons, of which I protest
to you by my salvation there was not one that had any
dependence or relation to you, so in all the passage of it did
I forbear to use any such person, who by furtherance of it
might violate any trust or duty towards you.

The reasons why I did not fore-acquaint you with it (to
deal with the same plainness I have used) were these:—I
knew my present estate less than fit for her. I knew (yet I
knew not why) that I stood not right in your opinion. I
knew that to have given any intimation of it had been to
impossibilitate the whole matter. And then, having these
honest purposes in our hearts and these fetters in our
consciences, methinks we should be pardoned if our fault
be but this, that we did not, by fore-revealing of it, consent
to our hindrance and torment.

Sir, I acknowledge my fault to be so great, as I dare scarce
offer any other prayer to you in mine own behalf than this,
to believe this truth,—that I neither had dishonest end nor
means. But for her, whom I tender much more than my
fortunes or life (else I would, I might neither joy in this
life nor enjoy the next), I humbly beg of you that she may
not, to her danger, feel the terror of your sudden anger.

I know this letter shall find you full of passion; but I
know no passion can alter your reason and wisdom, to
which I adventure to commend these particulars;—that it is
irremediably done; that if you incense my lord, you destroy
her and me; that it is easy to give us happiness, and that my
endeavours and industry, if it please you to prosper them,
may soon make me somewhat worthier of her.

If any take the advantage of your displeasure against me,
and fill you with ill thoughts of me, my comfort is that you
know that faith and thanks are due to them only that speak
when their informations might do good, which now it

cannot work towards any party. For my excuse I can say
nothing, except I knew what were said to you.

Sir, I have truly told you this matter, and I humbly
beseech you so to deal in it as the persuasions of Nature,
Reason, Wisdom, and Christianity shall inform you; and to
accept the vows of one whom you may now raise or scatter
—which are, that as my love is directed unchangeably upon
her, so all my labours shall concur to her contentment, and
to show my humble obedience to yourself.

Yours in all duty and humbleness,

J. Donne

From my lodging by the Savoy,
2nd February 1601 [2].
To the Right Worshipful Sir George More, Kt.[3]

But the astonished Sir George did not understand or appre-
ciate the distorted manners of his new son-in-law. Instead
he had him thrown into prison and deprived of his position.
The jailing depended on a doubtful legal technicality in the
marriage and was soon overthrown. The regaining of the
lost position, however, depended on personal influence and
was by no means rapidly recovered.

Ten years were to pass before Donne attained a position
resembling the one he lost by that dramatic marriage in
1601, and during most of those ten years the best he could
do by way of affirming the more conservative ideal of
marriage was to prove to himself that he could add to a
romantic marriage contract his own personal efforts to
provide a stable domestic household. This much he imme-
diately set about doing and loyally continued, regardless of
his financial circumstances. Those desperate years in which
Donne was essentially without a position were the decisive
years of his religious growth. They were the crisis of his
life, at once vocational and religious, spiritual and practical,
and they are the years with which I am particularly con-
cerned in this book.

3. Quoted from Gosse, *Life*, I, 100–102.

Some important things are known now about this period
which were unknown to Edmund Gosse when he wrote the
Life and Letters of John Donne, published in 1899, which
is still the standard biography.[4] R. C. Bald has clarified the

4. Izaak Walton's biography is still an indispensable source.
Gosse includes all but two of the *Letters* of 1651, but the edition
of Charles Edmund Merrill, Jr., published as *Letters to Severall
Persons of Honour by John Donne* (New York: Sturgis & Wal-
ton, 1910) includes some helpful notes. Augustus Jessop's *Life
of John Donne: Sometime Dean of St. Paul's A.D. 1621–1631*
(Boston: Houghton, Mifflin, 1897), though rightly superseded
by Gosse's *Life,* is unjustly neglected; Jessop is especially help-
ful for an American reader by placing Donne's youthful relation-
ships to the persons like Henry Goodyer and Lord Hay, who are
his lifelong friends, in a clear historical and personal context.
Many individual facts have been corrected since Gosse wrote, and
these have been taken into account, for books published prior to
1948, by Evelyn Simpson in her "Sketch of Donne's Life" (see
n. 2, above). The same seems to be true, for books published
prior to 1965, in Edward Le Compte's readable biography, *Grace
to a Witty Sinner: A Life of Donne* (New York: Walter, 1965),
but this book came to my attention only after my own manuscript
was complete, and I have been unable to make use of it or to
judge its accuracy or completeness. Other sources for Donne's
life as I have used them are referred to below, in this paragraph,
and *passim* throughout. A few other contributions to Donne
scholarship are particularly relevant to my own and, though they
have not entered into the writing of my text, deserve mention.
Something of the basic style of life which I have called "man-
nerist" is presented in Evelyn Hardy's biography, *Donne: A
Spirit in Conflict* (London: Constable, 1942), and the similarity
is even more evident in an article by Kathleen Raine (apparently
inspired by Evelyn Hardy's book), "John Donne and the Baroque
Doubt," *Horizon,* XI (1945), 371–95. Two good articles show
how the notion of Donne as a dissolute person in his youth,
completely different from the grave divine of his later years, has
gained its widespread acceptance: Allen R. Benham's "The Myth
of John Donne the Rake," *Philological Quarterly,* XX (1941),
465–73, and S. Ernest Sprott's "The Legend of Jack Donne the
Libertine," *University of Toronto Quarterly,* XIX (1950), 335–
53. Mr. Sprott's article seems to me better argued and is less de-
pendent on critical fashions. Neither one shows the consequences
of the collapse of this myth for Donne's middle life. The standard
bibliography is Geoffrey Keynes, *A Bibliography of Dr. John
Donne, Dean of Saint Paul's,* 3d ed. (Cambridge: At the Univer-
sity Press, 1958).

relationship Donne began with the Drury family in 1610, and Helen Gardner has argued that most of the Divine Poems, previously dated several years after his ordination, were written, instead, in 1608 and 1609.[5] Her dating of those poems has been decisive to the biographical vision I put forth here, and I have accepted it. But interpretative considerations have been more important in the plan, order, and contents of this book than considerations of dating. I make use of, but also dispute, the interpretations of Gosse, Gardner, and some others, especially Louis Martz and Frank Manley.[6] This gives me the advantage of all that they have seen and said and helps put into relief the edge of difference between us that is my own particular contribution.

That contribution depends upon bringing the externals of Donne's religious life into meaningful relationship to his inner life. Although Donne developed a great deal in depth, complexity, and clarity of religious life during the ten or fifteen years following his marriage, his life style did not change basically. He would experience life by uncovering, or creating, its polarities. Fastening his eye on one of those poles, he would rush upon it, and then he would turn around and rush upon the other one also. By doing it this way he would achieve in the end what he had been hoping for all along, the one world upon which the very possibility of polarity depends. Great personal activity became the principal means through which the reconciliation of the

5. R. C. Bald, *Donne and the Drurys* (Cambridge, Eng.: At the University Press, 1959); Helen Gardner, *John Donne: The Divine Poems,* printed from corrected sheets of the first edition, 2d ed. (Oxford: Oxford University Press, 1964 [1st ed, 1952]).
6. Louis Martz, *The Poetry of Meditation: A Study in English Religious Literature of the Seventeenth Century* (New Haven: Yale University Press, 1954); Frank Manley, *John Donne: "The Anniversaries"* (Baltimore: Johns Hopkins Press, 1963).

poles could be made.[7] In a world threatened with cleavages
so severe as to seem to destroy it, some heroic effort to hold
it together, even at the threat of personal bifurcation,
seemed justified. I hope to convey in the organization of my
own telling of the story something of Donne's own intense
effort to achieve the joining of one great pair of world
polarities. Therefore, having now begun this chapter with
the external crisis which dominated his life for the major
portion of the scope of this book and which led him
ultimately to ordination, I turn next to the earliest state-
ments of his inner life which bear on the externals of
religion. That requires us to move to a period in his life
whose dates are indefinite but which began a few years
prior to his marriage.

In his "Life of Dr. John Donne," Walton says that in
Donne's "eighteenth year" he had "betrothed himself to no
religion that might give him any other denomination than
a Christian. And reason and piety had both persuaded him
that there could be no such sin as schism, if an adherence to
some visible church were not necessary." [8] Walton's words
are a close paraphrase of Donne's own account in *Pseudo-
Martyr,* published in 1610. But there, the earlier period
talked about is by no means so crisply defined as Walton's
"eighteenth year," and it probably refers to the whole
period from his youth up until *Pseudo-Martyr,* published
when he was thirty-eight and probably written in the pre-
ceeding year. For Walton's "adherence to some visible
church" Donne's words were "binding my conscience to
any locall Religion." And for Walton's remark that Donne
had "betrothed himself to no religion that might give him

7. For a full scholarly treatment of the character and origin of
this spirit in Renaissance man see Frances A. Yates, *Giordano
Bruno and the Hermetic Tradition* (Chicago: University of Chi-
cago Press, 1964). I owe many insights into John Donne's life
and writings to this important book.
8. *Izaak Walton's Lives,* p. 19.

any other denomination than a Christian," Donne had written scornfully of those "who thinke presently, that hee hath no Religion, which dares not call his Religion by some newer name than *Christian.*" [9]

If, in talking of Donne's religion we mean his membership in a church, and if, by the term "church," we mean visible church, then we must probably conclude that Donne was both unchurched and nonreligious during that period. But we cannot make such assumptions. Walton, who was far from a subtle intellectual, uses almost casually the phrase "visible church," making the distinction with an invisible church a commonplace inference. And Donne himself seems to insist on a religion that may be called "Christian" but is nevertheless distinct from a "locall Religion." It would raise problems of meaning too difficult to handle here to assert that Donne's religion during his early to middle years was simply Christian, with membership in an invisible church; but that he chose some kind of invisible religion at the time of writing the third Satire, probably between 1594 and 1597, is beyond question. This much is clear from the contents of that poem and is generally accepted. In addition, I think it is not too much to say that the distinction between the visible and invisible churches was no mere antique theory to him but rather a tension actually experienced in his life.

What is not generally noted but is equally clear in the third Satire is the poet's interest in the revealed or visible forms of religious life and his dissatisfaction with invisible religion as a perpetual life condition. The presence of these elements in his attitude shows how inadequate an interpretation of this poem and of this period in his life is provided by the modern term "skepticism," which seems to persist in a stubbornly popular way in spite of the more correct view

9. The passage from *Pseudo-Martyr* is quoted from Evelyn M. Simpson, *Study of the Prose Works,* p. 188.

provided some years ago by Margaret L. Wiley.[10] It will
help to approach the religious meaning of the third Satire
by beginning with certain distinctions between visible and
invisible, or revealed and hidden, which affect its nonreli-
gious aspects.

Who speaks in this poem, and to whom is it addressed?
Let me set aside the notions that it may be considered to be
addressed to us or to someone outside the poet himself,
either real or imagined, and consider only the more usual
assumption—that the poet is speaking to himself. The
speaker and the auditor, so considered, are the two persons
of the one self of the poet. In such a view the auditor,
whose voice is largely, perhaps entirely, unheard, represents
the specific definable image of the poet, and the speaker
represents the self-reflexive center who is able to generate,
direct, see, or speak to such images. The first of these is the
persona of the visible, the second of the invisible, self.
Those two "selves" are implicated in the relationship be-
tween the "flesh" and the "soul" referred to in lines 40–42.
The speaker, addressing the auditor, says:

> Flesh (it selfes death) and joyes which flesh can taste,
> Thou lovest; and thy faire goodly soul, which doth
> Give this flesh power to taste joy, thou dost loath.[11]

10. In *The Subtle Knot* (Cambridge, Mass.: Harvard Univer-
sity Press, 1952), esp. Chap. IV, "John Donne and the Poetry of
Skepticism." Miss Wiley says of the key lines: "Donne's chief
fear was that men should come to rest in dogmatisms part-way
down the mountain-side, and so should cease struggling" (p.
126). However, she does not seem to notice Donne's skepticism
toward perpetual struggling in her analysis of these lines. Other
discussions of Donne's early religion are in Gosse's *Life,* the open-
ing chapter of Vol. I, esp. pp. 38–41, in Louis I. Bredvold, "The
Religious Thought of Donne in Relation to Medieval and Later
Traditions," *Studies in Shakespeare, Milton, and Donne,* Uni-
versity of Michigan Publications in Language and Literature, I
(New York: Macmillan, 1925), 193–232.
11. *The Poems of John Donne,* ed Herbert J. C. Grierson,
2 vols. (Oxford: Oxford University Press, 1912), I, 156. Other

The speaker here acts in sympathy with the soul and directs his voice to the auditor, whose affections are fastened upon the flesh, so that the discourse from speaker to auditor parallels the relationship of soul to flesh and represents the traditional medieval debate between body and soul. In Donne's debate, however, one voice is silent—the flesh, the external and visible self. Taken in this way the soul seems to say to the body, "You love yourself, but you should love me because I am the one who gives you the very power to love." Or to switch to the parallel terms of speaker and auditor, Donne's most inner voice says to the outer image of himself, "See how much I love you, that I give you my life power; why don't you love me?" Yet even though the flesh is accused and is silent, the speaker understands that external power of himself well enough to know that he gives that other part the power to love; he both speaks to it and understands it; the two are in some communication. Consequently, the distinction between them, though real and uncomfortable, is not ultimate.

But suppose the flesh *were* to love and cherish the soul as the soul seems to desire. How would it demonstrate that love? How would it speak? How would it, indeed, save in fleshly ways—open, visible, external ways, the ways in which the flesh can give glory to the soul *in the external world?* The speaker grasps that; it is why, with no intervening explanation, line 43 begins with the well-known admonition and reply upon which the remainder of the poem depends. "Seeke true religion," says the speaker; and this true religion means the external expression. But it is a quest hard even to begin, and the voice of the external self, audible here in the poem if anywhere, responds with quiet desperation, "O where?"

When the speaker then turns to describe the character of

quotes from the third Satire are from the same source, pp. 154–58.

the persons whom he pictures as representing the several
variants of the visible church, we find each a satiric type,
analogous to the type of the "flesh" in lines 40–42. Mir-
reus, Crantz, Graius, Phrygius, Graccus—each has found his
own "true religion," but each differs from the other and
none has the ring of authenticity. None really loves God
any more than the flesh loved the soul. Is God's power
truly to be found in any one of these particular figures?
That question is answered explicitly in the final couplet of
the poem:

> So perish Soules, which more chuse mens unjust
> Power from God claym'd, then God himselfe to trust.

It might seem that the speaker leaves himself in despair. Is
there no way for the visible reality of actually existing men
to become reconciled to the hidden power of God? Yes,
there is. The possibility of such a reconciliation is adum-
brated by the ambivalence and unity in the person ad-
dressed—he is both a specific image and the self-reflexive
power which gives that image life, and yet both are the
voices of one man. Furthermore, it is specifically indicated.
Why the tone of "Seeke true religion" if it cannot be
found? Let us examine those final lines more closely. They
reflect a hope implicit throughout the poem. They show
that a soul may expect to find "true religion" if it will
choose God's power directly. Does this then mean that
"true religion" is necessarily invisible? No. The speaker
hopes for a soul which will *"more* chuse" (my italics)
God's power than men's *unjust* claims to God's power; the
speaker's insistence on "unjust" does not exclude the possi-
bility of *just* claims to such power in some men.

The aspect of hope is indicated also in those central
passages of the poem which are so often quoted. "Doubt
wisely," the poet tells himself in lines 77–79, usually cited
to confirm Donne's "skepticism":

>   in strange way
> To stand inquiring right, is not to stray;
> To sleepe, or runne wrong, is.

"Doubt" by all means, but do it "wisely," the speaker insists. So also, to "stand inquiring" is acceptable, provided one does so in the right manner. This right inquiry and wise doubt are best understood by seeing how they parallel the better-known seventeenth-century concept of reason, in which the psychic stance indicated by the noun "reason" is commended as long as it moves in the direction secretly shown by the conscience. Right reason, in short, is reason moving in the right direction. Likewise, "inquiry" in Donne's "inquiring right" and "doubt" in his "doubt wisely" should be taken as final in themselves no more than reason is. Donne's "stand" implies direction and movement. The soul is not to "run wrong," but neither is it to "sleepe."

This tone of expectant movement is even clearer in the other well-known passage of the poem (ll. 79–84), the one containing the hill-of-truth metaphor. The speaker here clearly states that the attitude of uncertainty is not to be used to justify permanent postponement of the risk of ascent:

>   On a huge hill,
> Cragged, and steep, Truth stands, and hee that will
> Reach her, about must, and about must goe;
> And what the hills suddennes resists, winne so;
> Yet strive so, that before age, deaths twilight,
> Thy Soule rest, for none can worke in that night.

One may stand skeptical while he is young. He even should do so when the path is hard to see or difficult to ascend safely, but all of this earlier contemplation is for the sake of the final effort. Indeed, it is more important to make an attempt at the top, the speaker seems to say, than it is to wait until you can be absolutely sure to reach it.

The mode of movement proposed by the speaker describes one aspect of Donne's early religious life; one who would reach Truth, he says, "about must, and about must goe." These are words which seem to explicate the character of the wisdom in the "doubt" previously proposed. The way to go seeking the path consists of an indirect, circuitous, roundabout, or back-and-forth motion, somewhat like the winding serpentine ascent of Bernini's columns for the baldacchino in Saint Peter's cathedral, for example. It is not the kind of movement suggested by the simple verticals of the Greek columns widely imitated in the temples of our American Puritan forebears, who found a more direct way of removing themselves from the perils of a changing world than Donne did. At the time this poem was written, Donne was far from "death's twilight." The poem clearly tries to justify a temporary state suitable for a young man facing a complex religious situation. This temporary state consists in a kind of prowling around in the lower foothills of private and interior attitudes chiefly characterized by hesitation combined with expectancy.

What is Donne expecting? Two things, opposite but also apparently correlative. The soul must somehow discover a deeper and more direct access to the original and invisible source of power. Donne hopes to contact God directly. But the poet does not give up hope of discovering "true religion" according to some visible channel too—through men who may claim God's power justly.

Seeking God's power without visible intermediaries is usually considered Protestant, and seeking him through visible means, Catholic. But the labeling of Protestant and Catholic according to such superficial notions does not do justice to the subtlety of actual history. We must examine those matters more carefully if we will understand how these attitudes connect with the Protestant and, more importantly for Donne's earlier life, the Catholic positions of his own time. 1546483

Instead of merely identifying "invisible" with Protestant and "visible" with Catholic, let us begin by considering Protestant and Catholic views of the relationship between the so-called visible and invisible church. Discussion of such matters sharpened into separate attitudes in Reformation doctrinal disputes, where making a radical distinction between the visible and invisible church became identified as a Protestant position. The more Catholic a position one took, particularly in the earlier stages of the Reformation, the less he distinguished those two. To ascribe any great importance to a church invisible and separate from the public community was far from ordinary medieval doctrine; but, in the actual situation in England during Donne's lifetime, how was a Catholic to adhere to a visible church in fact? Where *was* the Catholic church visible? Certainly, lax enforcement of the penal laws enabled many Roman Catholics to remain absent from Anglican church services, and certainly also they could attend Mass and receive other ministrations from Roman Catholic priests. But the first of these they achieved by withdrawing from the most public and visible community of Christians anywhere available, and the second by hiding their worship services in private chapels, having them performed by secret priests, and communicating with Rome by smuggled messages and books.

Such a church does not represent the publicly visible medieval Catholicism that was Donne's family inheritance, and few English Christians could have been satisfied with the secrecy which this situation required. Those who clung to Rome had to accept it, but they did so only with great reluctance. To be sure, those who were willing to tune in to the new climate accommodated themselves more readily.

None did this better than the Jesuits, and their very success helped them to become more and more the official spokesmen for Rome. As they did so, they embraced the role of the secret priest more and more exuberantly—so much so that English popular sentiment, including even the more medieval-minded Catholics, turned against them. Thus the secret priest, the Jesuit—it was all one—became the chief target of the nervous fear of subversive plots in England at the opening of the century.[12]

Even the Jesuits, however, had not given in to this secrecy in England without a struggle. In earlier years they too had scorned it, and the Jesuitical devotion to the visible church in Donne's own family can be cited for an example. Donne's uncle, Jasper Heywood, after leaving the country at the time of Elizabeth's accession, returned in 1581 as the head of the Jesuit mission to England. There he was jailed and released into permanent exile in 1584/5 for behavior which Gosse said "outraged the commonest prudence" and Mrs. Simpson, in her sketch of Donne's life, called "foolishly ostentatious." [13] Most modern commentators agree. No doubt so did all convinced Protestants of that time, along with many cautious Catholics. But Jasper Heywood,

---

12. I make the concluding statements of this paragraph by inference from the rift between the seculars and regulars in England which became focused in the archpriest controversy. I assume that those Catholics more loyal to specifically English traditions would have favored the archpriest's authority (the seculars) against the Jesuits, as Queen Elizabeth did. Compare with this the summary in Martin Havran's *The Catholics in Caroline England* (Stanford: Stanford University Press, 1962), p. 84: "After the enactment of the Jacobean oath of allegiance in 1606, the quarrel among the clergy became more serious; some of the secular saw no harm in the oath, and a few took it to escape persecution. The archpriest Blackwell himself took the oath and advised others to do the same, even though Pope Paul V had forbidden it. Not surprisingly, the Pope punished Blackwell for disloyalty by stripping him of authority in 1608."

13. Gosse, *Life,* I, p. 13; Simpson, *A Study of the Prose Works of John Donne,* p. 14.

in making the church and his role in it so unmistakably visible, was simply continuing the medieval Christian tradition.

The actual situation for Catholicism in England at this time was an ecclesiastical anomaly, and it presented John Donne and all others of Roman Catholic birth with a curious dilemma. If Donne wanted to continue to follow the medieval Christian tradition of rendering the invisible Christ visible in the community of the church, how was he to do it? The visible was the Anglican, not the Roman Catholic. Should he then call himself a Roman Catholic? By doing this, he could affirm the medieval teaching; but this would preclude his actually becoming visible and would cut him off from his English heritage. Or should he call himself an Anglican? In this way, he could retain visible continuity with the same local community handed to him by his ancestors, but he would be cut off from the larger international Roman community and forced to receive a teaching which tended to separate the visible and invisible churches.

There were other practical alternatives, but none really solved the dilemma. One could leave the country, as some other Catholics had done; but that choice simply removed one more visible member from the medieval English church and certainly did not make it more Roman. Or, remaining in England, one could choose reckless visibility, as Donne's uncle had done; but this was bound to come to nothing different from going underground or abroad; one either met Jasper Heywood's fate or was jailed, perhaps to die, as his brother Henry did, of neglect or disease (not, by this time, in any grand visible spectacle of the defense of the faith). None of the alternatives, in short, made Roman Catholicism genuinely more visible in England. Each one, Jesuitical or non-Jesuitical, required the English Roman Catholic to abandon something very close to the heart of

medieval Christendom—the visible church planted every-
where, adapting itself to the forms of culture in whatever
place it grew.

In view of this dilemma, is it any wonder that Donne
chose the religious life of "wise skepticism" for a considera-
ble portion of his early years? But let us call it Christian
skepticism. In view of its outcome—as well as its sources
and its hope—we are justified in combining the Christian
and pagan terms for this early attitude. But its outcome was
not yet. Although Donne retained something of the medie-
val attitudes, he was no mere throwback. In order to be-
come a visible Christian in his own time he had also to
respond, somehow, to the character of religious life as it
was then lived. That religious climate required the aspirant
to live the inner life in some degree of separation from
traditional external expression—the very way that the so-
cial and political pressures were from his earliest years
already causing Donne to live.

CHAPTER III

MANNERISM

A new style of inner life came into religious culture in response to the new historical circumstances—a style which tended to isolate the inner life from external expression. This new inner life may be understood as one of the forms by which the invisible church was made an actual reality. Seeing it related to the invisible church usually suggests its Protestant character, and certainly it had been characteristic of Protestantism to find new meaning in human life by discovering God through personal spiritual means. Emphasis fell on faith, on conscience, on the private interpretation of Scripture, not on religious works, confession to the priest, or the bishop's interpretations of the church. The Protestant had made such individual experiences supplement, or even replace, the means of grace provided by the medieval Mass, where, above all, the reconciliation of inner and outer had been achieved.

But this new style of inner life was not restricted to Protestants. By Donne's time Catholicism had a well-developed strategy for a religious life of very similar character. This strategy is generally identified with the Counter Reformation and the Jesuits. In the ecclesiastical order, the Jesuits had leaped over the whole panoply of hierarchs to find all external meaning in only one of them—the pope. By thus simplifying that vast medieval structure, great power was released for the inner experience in the new religious life. The movement flourished in England as well as on the Continent, and among others it affected John Donne, as Martz and Gardner have shown.[1]

This new Catholic inner life was particularly widespread in the form prescribed by the *Spiritual Exercises.* Ignatius of Loyola specified the activity of each of three faculties of the psyche—memory, reason, and will—upon certain religious subjects, and especially on subjects derived from the Gospels. This threefold structuring of the psyche was inherited from Aristotle's treatise *On the Soul* by way of a simplification made in Saint Augustine's *On the Trinity.* Here and elsewhere in this study I use the term "psyche," transliterated from Aristotle's (and the New Testament's) Greek, interchangeably with the English "soul." In Donne's time "soul" was the ordinary English equivalent of the Greek, but it has now lost its force as referring to psychic phenomena. "Psyche," however, has been reborn in this older sense in modern depth psychology and is therefore more accurate.

However, the Counter Reformation forms of the new inner life were far more varied than can be indicated by the

1. Louis Martz, *The Poetry of Meditation: A Study in English Religious Literature of the Seventeenth Century* (New Haven: Yale University Press, 1954); Helen Gardner, *John Donne: The Divine Poems,* 2d ed. (Oxford: Oxford University Press, 1964). Much of what I have to say about the Ignatian tradition in this chapter and elsewhere in this book had its source in Martz's book. My own studies of that tradition can be seen in my dissertation, *The Meditative Life of Christ: A Study of the Background and Structure of Jeremy Taylor's "The Great Exemplar"* (Ann Arbor, Mich.: University Microfilms, 1959).

Spiritual Exercises alone. They included many schemes for "meditation" or "mental prayer," as these intense, systematic forms of cultivating the inner life were often called, including also various methods for performing a "mental communion." This latter was evidently designed for persons who were totally deprived of the ministrations of the visible church and was therefore specifically suited to Catholics living in Protestant lands. That the new movement separated inner life from outer expression is particularly evident in comparing the "mental communion" with the medieval Mass, but all of the private mental disciplines worked in the same direction. Through this largely Jesuit emphasis on a detached discipline of the inner life, the medieval focus on the intimate union of the invisible power of God joined to his visible and material presence in one specific definable center tended to disappear in Catholicism as well as in Protestantism.

But this separation was not so much a Catholic or a Protestant phenomenon as a world phenomenon. I use the term "world" here, as I did in Chapter I, to signify the general cultural milieu apprehended in John Donne's time. As a world phenomenon the religious community came to represent the inner, and the rest of the world the outer, life; and this was truer, the more outcast the religious community was. The deep cultivation of the inner life naturally will develop more if one's energies and abilities are thwarted in the outer world. Thus, while they were a vital but repressed group, the Puritans cultivated an inner life very similar to the Catholic meditation. They differed by being more preoccupied with the figures of the Old than the New Testament and in preferring biblical to Aristotelian categories for the experiences of the psyche.

In order for this repression to produce a healthful development of the personality, it is necessary to gain psychic depth without losing contact with the external world.[2] A person may separate his inner life from the outer world as much as he likes and make that the style of his existence, pushing both sides as far apart as he wishes to discover the separate character of each. In doing so, he may stretch, warp, dislocate, the simpler, older, more natural, or more direct modes of going between the inner and outer worlds, but he may not destroy that path utterly. He may not snap the invisible band between them by which they can be reconciled back into their oneness, their "original" wholeness.

Human communication is the indispensable agent of this reconciliation. Though its modes may change from age to age, its reality must continue. Comparing the more medieval modes with those developed in Donne's time, we see that the earlier modes emphasized oral (audible) while the newer ones emphasized written (visible) communication.[3] Oral communication continued into the later period, of course, but it developed characteristic new forms, chief among which was the sermon. Less intimate, direct, and personal, the new sermon was also more passionate and more rational than its medieval counterpart. It had to

2. See, for example, "Anima and Animus" in *The Basic Writings of C. G. Jung,* ed., with an introduction, by Violet S. de Laszlo, Modern Library edition (New York: Random House, 1959), pp. 158–82, esp. p. 175: "No adaptation can result without concessions to both worlds [the inner and the outer]." The writings of C. G. Jung, principally from this volume and from the selection entitled *Psyche and Symbol,* ed. Violet S. de Laszlo (New York: Doubleday, Anchor Books, 1958), have strongly affected the character of my psychological analysis throughout this study. I have also consulted the *Collected Works of C. G. Jung,* ed. Herbert Read, Michael Fordham, and Gerhard Adler, Bollingen Series XX (Princeton: Princeton University Press), Vol. VII (2d ed., 1966) and Vol. VIII (1960).

3. For the importance of the visible in the newer movements of the Renaissance see Walter J. Ong, S.J., *Ramus: Method, and the Decay of Dialogue* (Cambridge, Mass.: Harvard University Press, 1958).

develop this greater power because it crossed a greater distance. But whether written or oral, old or new, centric or eccentric, the channel between inner and outer had to be found.

A disjunct inner and outer life, whose resolution, dislocated rather than absent, is discovered in practice by extraordinary individual power, is one of the principal patterns of "mannerism" as I shall use the term in this book.[4] As is generally true of advanced movements, mannerism was chiefly discovered and practiced by the intelligentsia. *The Burial of Count Orgaz* by El Greco (see frontispiece) illustrates the mannerist disjunction in painting. The hidden juncture between the lower and upper portions of the painting is found in the ghostly, infant-like soul of Count Orgaz ascending through the womblike passage in the center of the painting. This moving soul-figure mirrors the psychic movement of the viewer, who unifies, with difficulty, the depth memories [5] of the faith and the surface of historic reality round about him. However dislocated from the painting, the psychic power of the man viewing it is the

---

4. See n. 4 in Chapter I, above, and my own text at that point.
5. I use the term "depth memories" because it suggests depth psychology. There are two aspects of the psyche: the superficial (my "surface") or more fully conscious awarenesses, and the deeper (my "depth") or more unconscious. I am trying to suggest that the viewer will have two kinds of memories as he views the picture: the memory of his everyday experience, with its living, historical personages and its events, like death, and a deeper, more remote, memory made for him by the church, in language, liturgy, and visual or graphic art, of the so-called "heavenly" persons and figures whom El Greco places in the upper half of the painting. What I, following depth psychology, place lower, El Greco places higher; but his infant-like soul-figure pictures the reconciliation of that paradox, too: in the ordinary realm of existence we understand death as a going-down, but in the special way suggested by the painting, death (and the unconscious—or more "spiritual"—life) is really a going-up; hence, the body goes *down* to its grave, but the soul—no longer tied to the earthly body—goes up.

vital counterpart of the resolving center in the image of the soul of Count Orgaz.

To be sure, some mannerist paintings are entirely devoted to picturing the resolution between the poles rather than the poles themselves, but even in these paintings the resolution is not pictured in any ladder-like sequence. The form between the extremes is, rather, serpentine or sinewy, twisted, stretched, or elongated out of its natural proportions, especially between the upper and lower portions of the painting or sculpture. It is the kind of thing that can be seen in El Greco's *Laocoön* or Parmigianino's *Madonna with the Long Neck.*

The basic pattern had many variants. The most important of these variants for our study is that in which the disjunction between inner and outer is reflected as a disjunction within the inner life alone, which I shall call the mannerist inner life. The mannerist inner life was not felt as an ordered and harmonious hierarchy of three or more faculties of the soul, as they were shown in the *Spiritual Exercises.* Rather it was felt as two—apparently separated—faculties of the soul, reflecting the disjunction between the inner and outer life.

When the mannerist inner life took its terms out of the Aristotelian categories, the result was likely to be a pair labeled intellect and emotion (or reason and will, or judgment and passion), the very terms which are our own familiar language of everyday psychology and are still felt to be more or less in conflict with each other. In Donne's time it might also have taken its terms out of biblical categories, in which case it was likely to come out as "flesh" and "soul," as it did in lines 40–43 of the third Satire. Note that, contrary to modern expectations, both of these terms function as categories of the inner life, not the second one only. But it might also take one term from the Aristotelian and one from the biblical tradition, coming up then in the form of such a disjunct pair as reason and faith, or thought and prayer. This model of the inner life reflects the external polarity of classical and Christian or, more broadly, secular and sacred. In such pairs the rational or upper level of the psyche is expressed by the term associated with the classical tradition and will seem to be more learned and more sophisticated—but also more superficial. The religious term, on the other hand, represents the emotional or lower level of the psyche and seems to be more primitive, deeper, or more profound than the secular term but also vague, mysterious, and possibly dangerous.

This new duality can be understood as part of the effort of the Renaissance-Reformation to simplify the complexities of medieval Scholasticism, or it can be said to represent the challenge which the new "simpler" Platonism was making to the quiddities of the prevailing Aristotelianism. Of course a dual inner life was not an invention of the Renaissance-Reformation any more than were the great number of other dualities of the late sixteenth and early seventeenth centuries. It was present in the late medieval tradition too, but it was represented there in a different mode. The psychic duality of reason and faith constitutes the very substance of the *Summa,* for example. But the heart of the *Summa* lies in the smooth and nearly indistinguishable continuity between them, not in their apparent disjunction. In Saint Thomas, as in Dante also, though a certain duality is everywhere implied, we are not led to attend to the twoness. We are made to focus on the much greater multiplicity of discretely numbered steps or levels connecting these two. Thus, in Saint Thomas, the numbered questions and answers constitute these steps, and, in Dante, they can be seen in the various levels of Hell. We know, of course, in the back of our minds that these multiple divisions represent steps between something and something, but our attention is almost entirely confined to the hierarchical rapprochement; this alone is expressly visible. But the contrary is true in the language and attitude of John Donne and in the mannerist style generally, where all the light is thrown on the two extremes, the rapprochement being only inferred, suggested, or intuited. Or, the rapprochement may be transferred to another plane of reality related in a polar way to the one in which the lighted pair is found, as when we consider that the viewer of El Greco's *Burial of Count Orgaz* himself is to experience the resolution which the artist only dimly pictures. In mannerist art or writing of this type we can hardly see how one goes from one of a pair of opposites to the other, so nearly lost, so dark and obscure, is the way between.

This mannerist duality will be found in the various psychic pairs of the inner life, as well as in numerous such pairs in the outer world; each pair reflecting the disjunction between inner and outer. In the introduction to *Pseudo-Martyr* (1610) Donne gives his own account of the dual psychic movements which finally resolved his conflict about the visible church.

In *Pseudo-Martyr* Donne's term for his earlier psychic state is "irresolution"; it is the same state he called "wise doubt" or "right inquiry" in the third Satire. And this term of Donne's shows again how poor an interpretation the modern "skepticism" makes for that earlier hesitation. Unlike our "skepticism," which suggests a stable and fixed position of its own, "irresolution" distinctly implies the expectation of some future movement of resolution. Donne begins:

> Although I apprehended well enough that this irresolution not onely retarded my fortune, but also bred some scandall, and endangered my spirituall reputation, by laying me open to many mis-interpretations; yet all these respects did not transport me to any violent and sudden determination, till I had, to the measure of my poore wit and judgement sur-

vayed and digested the whole body of Divinity, contro-
verted betweene ours and the Romane Church.[6]

The function of his earlier irresolution, he seems to say,
was to provide time to apply his "wit and judgement" to
theological study, that is, to use his intellect. The emotional
side of his psyche is adumbrated in the form of threat or
danger: he needs time for study lest he resolve the issue by
"violent and sudden determination."

But this theological study was not to be undertaken in
such a way as to give no place to the more primitive and
passionate side of his inner life, as the other part of the
passage goes right on to insist:

> In which search and disquisition, that God, which awak-
> ened me then, and hath never forsaken me in that industry,
> as he is the Authour of that purpose, so is he a witnes of
> this protestation; that I behaved my selfe, and proceeded
> therin with humility, and diffidence in my selfe; and by
> that, which by his grace, I tooke to be the ordinary meanes,
> which is frequent praier, and equall and indifferent
> affections.[7]

The word "affections" clues us in to the psychic faculty
represented by "praier," and after the demonstrations of
Martz and Gardner we must suppose that his "praier and
. . . affections" constituted actually experienced psychic
activity and were not the mere verbal convention that
modern intellectuals have often supposed.

But if proceeding with intellectual study alternating with
frequent intervals for "praier, and equal and indifferent
affections," was his procedure for climbing the hill of truth,
what has happened to the third faculty of the soul, mem-

6. Evelyn M. Simpson, *A Study of the Prose Works of John Donne*, 2d ed. (Oxford: Oxford University Press, 1948), p. 188.
7. *Ibid.*

ory? Does its disappearance mean that Donne actually had
no "memory"—no imaginative life—during this period? Of
course not. And, indeed, the hidden part functions as the
principal path along which motion proceeds. But unless this
part had been suppressed from the account of his inner life,
the typical polar pattern could not have been revealed as
the form of his psyche. The suppression simply means that
it is displaced. It functions here in another realm which is
polarly connected to the inner life—the external world
itself, the visible forms and images of the historical church.
The mere fact that Donne omits it from his account in the
passage I have cited does not produce any genuine obscu-
rity. Who, in reading *Pseudo-Martyr,* could fail to have the
visible church of Donne's own time in mind during the
whole of his reading? The images of the English church of
his early family experiences lay behind all the intellection
and affection of the years Donne alludes to in this passage.
When Donne joined the Anglican church, he made those
memories active. Of course the Anglican church was not
merely the result of his own personal psychic activity; it
was also the result of the activity of those many other men
who, like Donne himself, had chosen to join their lives to
it. Each of them, especially the more able among them, by
joining it, moved it, and they were each also, of course,
moved by it.

Whatever could have led Gosse to say that Donne's
conversion to Anglicanism at this time was chiefly "intel-
lectual"? It could not have been because of Walton's selec-
tive citation of this passage, for in his *Life and Letters*
Gosse, unlike Walton, quotes the whole of it—"wit" and
"affections" both.[8] Gosse believed this because he was a
modern man—hence a man of divided sensibility. His

8. Gosse, *Life,* I, 250.

blindness to the "intellectual passions"[9] in Donne's poetry has long been recognized, but his blindness to the same quality in Donne's religion has gone largely unnoticed. Fortunately, we are now in a position to recognize both.

For Gosse, the sensibility divided itself, so that scholarship was intellectual, while religion and poetry were both emotional. Anything that threatened these neat categories was synonymous with error. To allow emotion to enter scholarship was bad; Gosse thought it Walton's chief fault. But to allow intellect to enter poetry or religion was equally bad. The witty element in Donne's poetry was regularly an excrescence to Gosse, and so also was it in his religion. Since *Pseudo-Martyr* was chiefly theological, which to a man of Gosse's generation and training meant "intellectual," it must be bad religion. Hence Donne could not have been really "converted" at this time. Of course Gosse could see that Donne had emotional qualities in his religious life, and he found them with particular clarity in the Divine Poems. But *Pseudo-Martyr* was dated 1610 on its title page; the Divine Poems were undated. When Gosse added these facts together with a clue from the early evangelical, Izaak Walton, who, although he was closer in time to Donne than Gosse was, was already out of touch with mannerist attitudes, the solution emerged: Donne had two separate lives, familiarly known to all Donne students as Jack Donne and John Donne. Gosse did it up more thoroughly than Walton. Walton showed us a sacred Donne and a

9. I borrow this term from a chapter title in Michael Polanyi's important book *Personal Knowledge: Towards a Post-Critical Philosophy* (Chicago: University of Chicago Press, 1958). Polanyi's recognition that passion, as well as all the important aspects of man's psychic and bodily existence, is involved in the intellectual life of science is an important sign of the distance we have now traveled from the divisive attitudes characteristic of modernity.

secular Donne; Gosse shows us two separate sacred Donnes replete with two separate conversions, the first one intellectual and false, the second one emotional and true. Gosse's use of the term "conversion" is not only a reflection of the nineteenth-century evangelical tradition but belongs also to the general tradition of great cleavages upon which the whole of modernity was founded. Thus the radical separation of secular from sacred, Protestant from Catholic, modern from medieval was as much a part of the divided sensibility of Gosse's time as was the separation between intellect and emotion.

But Gosse's version of Donne's religious experience must be abandoned now that Miss Gardner has shown us with compelling textual and manuscript evidence that the (emotional) Divine Poems were written during the same period in which Donne was doing the (intellectual) study for *Pseudo-Martyr.* We now can see, as he himself stated clearly in *Pseudo-Martyr,* that reason and emotion are yoked together in the "religious" John Donne just as they are in the "literary" John Donne. And in neither was his memory inoperative, though it may have been hidden from view, as it is in the passage we have studied here. All of Donne's psychic faculties joined together during these middle years of his ascent up the hill of truth. And so also did Catholic and Protestant join—or perhaps I should say with greater accuracy that Donne refused to sunder them. In Donne's life and writings the medieval and modern join, and so do poetry and religion, in the same movements and in the same experiences—though never without duress, strain, and tension in the inner life and corresponding transformation, convolution, and distortion in the outer. All these anguished reconciliations were part of the mannerist pattern.

What I am calling mannerist style is reminiscent of

Johnson's "metaphysical" style: "a combination of dissimilar images . . . yoked by violence together." [10] Some readers, no doubt, will want to know why I prefer the term "mannerism." I conceive of two distinctions upon which I base this preference. The first of these is related to the over-all character of mannerism as I have explained it in Chapter I and in the first part of this chapter: mannerism is not fundamentally an aesthetic style; it is a style of life, and in this style of life the literary or other arts may have a meaningful function. The term has arisen out of studies in art history, where it is not, however, confined to some strictly aesthetic realm but is related to religious, social, political, and literary history as well.[11] I connect the term also with depth psychology and certain aspects of existentialism and phenomenology. This large number of associations shows that mannerism is a reconciliatory word. "Metaphysical style," however, is a term whose meaning is almost entirely confined to literary contexts and discussions. Some readers will prefer it for that reason. But I conceive that the modern tradition of fragmented learning which supports both that term and its carefully circumscribed functions serves to heighten and encourage an exclusively linguistic or literary approach to John Donne which is false to the genuine function and significance of his life and art. In Donne's time metaphysics was still a language by which one expressed the real and serious concerns of one's actual existence as a man, while the term "metaphysical style" in modern literary studies means a linguistic technique. To see Donne's writings as a set of examples illustrating the metaphysical style and to turn them therefore into one of the

10. Samuel Johnson, "Abraham Cowley," in *Lives of the English Poets*, Everyman's Library ed. (London: J. M. Dent, 1925), II, 11.
11. See n. 4, p. 43, above.

many sleights of hand in the writer's bag of tricks, no matter how brilliant its practitioner may therefore appear, seem to me to be a depraved use of learning.

My second distinction is more closely related to the nature of mannerist inner life, as I have called it (pp. 44 f.). Under the pressure of the Enlightenment, when the term "metaphysical" was coined for Donne's writing, reason and emotion were isolated from each other far more decisively than the two ever were for Donne. The romantic climate which succeeded the Enlightenment, though it re-discovered emotion, did no more than the age which pre-ceded it to reconcile emotion with reason. One effect of the romantic climate we have already seen in Gosse. These two movements have so dominated modernity that "metaphysi-cal," like many other terms referring to inner realities, has been forced to fit either an exclusively rational or an exclusively emotional model. The rational model seems to have been chosen. Thus, the "metaphysical style" seems to be fundamentally a form of intelligence, an exercise of irony and wit. But such a notion for John Donne is no more than a half-truth.

Another term, recently made current by Martz and Gardner as a basic concept for interpreting Donne, is "med-itative." This has been a necessary corrective to "metaphysi-cal," and the meditative interpretation of Donne is very important to this study. Nevertheless, it is inadequate. Like the term "metaphysical," it fails to supply rich enough connections to the stuff of actual life. "Meditative" seems to suggest some kind of meaning which can be explicated solely by reference to Donne's inner life, cut off from external life and history. Furthermore, in its actual usage by Martz in his discussions of Donne, and to a lesser extent by Gardner also, the meditative is made to signify little more than the structure of literary form, to uncover its bare bones. No doubt this narrow usage of the term is the result of pressure from the technical orientation prevailing in humanistic studies, especially in this country, but it may also be a safeguard against the explosive power of permitting the existential implications of mental prayer to become genuinely operative in the way that metaphysical wit did for a generation of literary students. And when the existential power of the meditative is permitted to emerge —in the present climate of American education, where this is very novel—the result is to emphasize too much the emotional or subrational, just as the "metaphysical" approach too much emphasizes the rational. This point may not be entirely convincing until one compares the effects of the two types of interpretation among groups of sensitive and open students.

Moreover, insofar as the meditative represents a specific structural technique, an important shortcoming is introduced. "Meditative" does not really fit Donne's writing as well as "metaphysical" did; and, what "metaphysical" did, "mannerism" does better. The simplest way to reveal this problem is to consider the numerical conflict between the two earlier concepts. "Metaphysical" always described two things yoked together (e.g., reason and love), while "meditative" describes three (memory, reason, and love); and how can one and the same literary type be simultaneously both double and triple in form?

In mannerism it can be. The similarity of the mannerist to the metaphysical "yoking of the opposites" has already been mentioned. Consider now the mannerist in relation to the triple meditative structure: mannerism simplifies the threefold categories of the soul as found in the *Spiritual Exercises* by assimilating three into two. It distorts the smoothness of the movement between them by seeing principally their disjunction rather than their harmony; and yet, in mannerist art, the omitted third remains dimly apparent, as we have seen. Repressed, held out of sight, or displaced into a realm related to the other two by polar disjunction, this dimly apparent third will generally function as the path of reconciliation between the other two. In mannerism the suppressed third of the threefold meditative pattern becomes the yoke which "by violence," as Johnson said, conjoins the remaining two.

Donne was neither an Enlightenment wit nor a romantic spirit; he was both; he was a mannerist man. He was mannerist in the relationship of his inner to his outer life, in the relationship of the poles of his inner life to each other, and in the reconciliation he tried to make in the growing polarities of the outer world itself. The mannerist concept requires us to understand the functions of literary language as joining inner to outer life. We must see language as a function of both psyche and soma and of the polarities discoverable in either of these alone. To create the possibility of doing so, this book mixes biography and literary analysis, or external and internal history. Though I must, in the nature of the subject—because Donne himself did so, and because of the exigencies of the act of writing—bring now one pole into focus, now another, and yet again talk of mixtures or reconciliations, still the mannerist mode of relationship is always the point: the oneness in which the two are reconciled. Does the term "mannerist mode" suggest a static and fixed condition? To that extent my phrasing is bad. The oneness of the mannerist mode can be understood rightly only when it can be felt to represent the halting, lurching, leaping, intuitive flow of a deeply experienced life movement participating in the stream of actual history. He who would ascend the hill of truth "about must and about must goe."

Between the time of his writing the third Satire, when he was doubtful about the external church, and of his declaration for the Anglican church in 1610, Donne must have experienced this movement. In order to see just how, we must study some of those intervening years in detail. The sources are few, and the reliability of some are doubtful, so our conclusions must remain to some extent hypothetical. Perhaps they may be tested by how well they fit the pattern that seems to emerge from the over-all story.

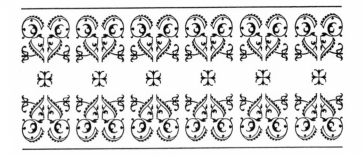

CHAPTER IV

"RESOLUTION" DECLINED

S hortly after June 22, 1607, when John Donne was
thirty-five, poor, and without other friends to help him,
Thomas Morton offered him a benefice in the Church of
England. Morton had just been made dean of Gloucester
and had some such gifts at his disposal. He had known
Donne earlier in the role of what we might call research
assistant, a secretary working intimately with him in prepa-
ration of some writing. Morton had been commissioned by
King James to prepare some pamphlets against those who
refused the Oath of Obedience, chiefly Roman Catholics,
though Anabaptists and some others maintained a separa-
tist stance on this matter also.[1] Morton's aptness for and
success in working with the recusants is eloquently de-
scribed by the character Gosse gives him, a man

1. Gosse, *Life,* I, 150.

specially distinguished at this time for his minglement of the serpent and the dove in dealing with Roman Catholics. His public conference with the Romish Recusants at York in 1601, and his subsequent courtesy to his opponents, had made his talents in this direction universally acknowledged, and for the next ten years Morton was pre-eminently the persuader and proselytiser of weak-kneed Catholics.[2]

As Walton reports the story,[3] Morton seems to have understood well Donne's ambitions and his poverty when he urged him to "waive your Court hopes, and enter into holy orders," and held out the offer of the benefice. Furthermore, by doing so, he now brought the problems of Donne's vocation to a powerful focus and forced him to

2. *Ibid.*, p. 161.
3. Walton's record of this encounter appears in his "Life" of Donne for the first time in the revision of 1658, some 51 years after the event and 18 years after Donne's death. The passage is slightly revised in the 1670 and 1675 versions. Although Walton is rightly noted for his inaccuracies of fact, his is the fullest account of this event, and there is some indication that it is more accurate than much else in Walton. The basic story is confirmed by Richard Baddeley; see the passages quoted in Evelyn Simpson, *A Study of the Prose Works of John Donne,* 2d ed. (Oxford: Oxford University Press, 1948), p. 25. Of Donne's reply to Morton Mrs. Simpson says that it was "reported by Morton himself" and that, although "Gosse points out that the wording of this speech has not the peculiar ring of Donne's style, . . . no doubt need therefore be thrown on the general trustworthiness of the narrative. The speeches which Walton records are clearly not reported verbatim, but represent the general substance of Donne's conversations reproduced in Walton's own phrases, though the use of the first person is retained throughout" (*A Study of the Prose Works,* p. 23). Walton says he had the story from firsthand contact with Morton. He must have worked from a document supplied by Morton, as Gosse thought, or from notes and recollections of a personal visit with him, as David Novarr thinks just as likely. Novarr places Walton's visit with Morton in London, before 1648 (David Novarr, *The Making of Walton's "Lives"* [Ithaca: Cornell University Press, 1958], pp. 71–73). The quotations from Walton in this chapter are from pages 26–28 of the Nelson Classics edition (Walton's revision of 1675).

make a decision. Even before Morton had had any offer to go along with it, he had attempted to sway Donne in just that way: "You know I have formerly persuaded you to waive your Court hopes, and enter into holy orders" is the full context of Walton's record of this part of Morton's speech. But these latest persuasions came "with this reason added to my former request," as Morton said, now offering the benefice, equal in value to his own deanery.

Three conditions were explicit in the choice if we assume Walton's report to be correct: Donne must become ordained, he must accept the proffered benefice, and he must give up his court hopes. A fourth is implicit in the first: he must declare himself unequivocally an Anglican.

The offer was related to both the financial and the spiritual tension in Donne's life. Coming as it did after he and Morton had spent considerable time together preparing arguments against stubborn Catholics, and when Donne had little money and not much in the way of prospects for more, it must have suggested to him an excellent opportunity. If the qualities implicit in the mannerist life style, as outlined in the last chapter, are rightly to be understood as John Donne's, it may be hard to see how he could have refused such a nice resolution of his inner and outer life in one decision.

But he did refuse. Why?

Morton made his offer to Donne only after eliciting a promise from him that he would not respond immediately, requesting "that you shall not return me a present answer, but forbear three days, and bestow some part of that time in fasting and prayer; and after a serious consideration of what I shall propose, then return to me with your answer." After hearing the proposal, "Mr. Donne's faint breath and perplexed countenance give a visible testimony of an inward conflict; but he performed his promise, and departed without returning an answer till the third day."

Walton then puts the account of Donne's reply in a long speech, which I shall present here piecemeal in order to make my interpretations. He will not accept the offer, begins Donne, because

> some irregularities of my life have been so visible to some men, that though I have, I thank God, made my peace with Him by penitential resolutions against them, and by the assistance of his grace banished them my affections; yet this, which God knows to be so, is not so visible to man as to free me from their censures, and it may be that sacred calling from a dishonour.

Donne's reasoning here balances external and internal considerations against each other; the decisive weight here falls upon his *apparent* character: the irreligious man seen by others regardless of his known inner changes. For Donne, inner character alone was not enough to qualify a man for "that sacred calling." His hidden character must be made sufficiently "visible to man" to gain society's approval. Part of the actual meaning of his life, Donne seems to say, derives from its stamp upon the minds of other men.

In the reasoning which follows, the internal difficulties dominate the balancing act between inner and outer:

> And besides, whereas it is determined by the best of casuists that God's glory should be the first end, and a maintenance the second motive to embrace that calling, and though each man may propose to himself both together, yet the first may not be put last without a violation of conscience, which he that searches the heart will judge. And truly my present condition is such that if I ask my own conscience whether it be reconcilable to that rule, it is at this time so perplexed about it, that I can neither give myself nor you an answer. You know, sir, who says, "Happy is that man whose conscience doth not accuse him for that thing which he does."

We will not understand this passage rightly if we take the conflict between "God's glory" and a "maintenance" to be the precise form of Donne's problem of conscience. This way of talking is the result of what we may call the instructed conscience, as the reference to the "best of casuists" indicates. A casuist was a spiritual director, a person more or less highly skilled in problems of inner conflict, and was thus somewhat analogous to a modern psychotherapist. Nevertheless, the instructed conscience is apparently of considerable meaning to Donne. To consider it with some care in this place will help us not only to understand this in itself but also will give us a language in which to discuss the invisible conscience.

Who is (or are) this (or these) "best of casuists"? I do not know. However, close parallels to the language here can be found in the *Spiritual Exercises* of Loyola, and I think it likely that Donne consulted the *Exercises* or, more likely, some other writers of the Ignatian tradition [4] before returning his answer to Morton. Morton had specifically asked Donne to devote part of the three days of serious consideration of his offer to prayer. If at any time in his life he had a specific reason to turn to the tradition of the *Spiritual Exercises,* it would have been now, because that method of prayer was specifically intended to resolve inner conflicts over religious vocation. Moreover, Donne's familiarity with that tradition, as shown by Martz and Gardner, is identified with the literature written during the four years following Morton's proposal. Nowhere is the influence of

4. Probably Spanish. See Gosse, *Life,* II, 176–78, for some evidence and discussion of Donne's interest in Spanish divinity. A large number of the books in Donne's library, including many by Spanish authors, have been identified and are described in the standard bibliography by Geoffrey Keynes, *A Bibliography of Dr. John Donne, Dean of Saint Paul's,* 3d ed. (Cambridge, Eng.: At the University Press, 1958).

the *Spiritual Exercises* clearer than in the Holy Sonnets, which Miss Gardner dates within two years of the offer.[5]

The vocational intention is everywhere implied in the *Spiritual Exercises,* but it is specifically focused in the period set aside by Loyola for "The Election." The life situations about which one might rightly seek to make an "election" included two of the three matters explicitly identified in Morton's offer: taking orders and accepting a benefice. Under the "Consideration for the purpose of taking knowledge of the matters about which an Election ought to be made," the *Spiritual Exercises* reads:

> There are some things which fall under an immutable Election, such as are the priesthood, matrimony, etc.; there are others which fall under a mutable Election, as, for instance, accepting or relinquishing benefices, accepting or renouncing temporal goods.[6]

Since this Catholic form of "election" had to do with making an actual choice in the world, the question of one's will was crucial. But the place of man's will in the religious life is by no means so simple as the distinction between Catholic freedom and Calvinist determinism usually suggests. Saint Ignatius' "Election" seems to require man's own

5. See Helen Gardner, *John Donne: The Divine Poems,* 2d ed. (Oxford: Oxford University Press, 1964), pp. xxxvii–lv. To Miss Gardner's arguments add that Martz notes the likelihood that the Holy Sonnets were the outgrowth of Donne's struggles with the problem of "Election" (Louis Martz, *The Poetry of Meditation: A Study in English Religious Literature of the Seventeenth Century* [New Haven: Yale University Press, 1954], pp. 218–20).

6. *The "Spiritual Exercises" of Saint Ignatius of Loyola, Translated from the Spanish, With a Commentary and a Translation of the "Directorium in Exercitia,"* by W. H. Longridge, S.S.J.E., 5th ed. (London: A. R. Mowbray, 1955; 1st ed., 1919), p. 127 (cited hereafter as *Spiritual Exercises*).

will to determine the religious course of his life, while the Calvinist election seems to deny the relevance of man's will utterly; but both characterizations are superficial. In the Calvinist election to salvation, God's will is indeed generally held completely to determine man's will; but Calvinism never supposed that, when this had happened, man's will was in any conflict with God's will. What serious Calvinist, considering himself elected, also considered himself consciously and actively bent on electing Satan's will in his conscientious life choices? For a Calvinist, to have submitted to God's will meant having something happen to his own will so that it could no longer be distinguished from God's. No doubt, man had a will and God had a will; but for the elect those two were one.

Something similar is described also in the *Spiritual Exercises.* In order to arrive at a proper election the performant must begin by ridding himself of all "inordinate affections," a process and a phrase which Saint Ignatius tirelessly reiterates.[7] When these have been successfully dealt with, he will have reached the highly important state of being "indifferent." [8] Then, and then only, is he in a proper state to experience God's will for him and to make the right election because then only will his choice and God's choice for him be one and the same. Thus the election of the *Spiritual Exercises,* like the Calvinist election by God, envisages an experience in which God's will determines man's choices.

The pertinent passage in the *Spiritual Exercises* reads:

> That we should make ourselves indifferent to all created things, in all that is left to the liberty of our free-will, and is not forbidden; in such sort that we do not for our part wish for health more than sickness, for wealth more than

7. *Spiritual Exercises,* pp. 4, 24, 127, for example.
8. *Ibid.,* p. 42.

poverty, for honour more than dishonour, for a long life more than a short one, and so in all other things; desiring and choosing only that which leads us more directly to the end for which we were created.[9]

Another passage in the *Spiritual Exercises* may be taken as an explanation of how those who were performing the exercises were to "make [themselves] indifferent":

> For the same purpose, namely, that the Creator and Lord may more surely work in His creature, if perchance such a soul is inordinately affected and inclined to anything, it will be very profitable for it to stir itself up and employ all its forces to arrive at the contrary of that to which it is wrongly affected. Thus, if it be desirous to seek and possess some office or benefice, not for the honour and glory of God our Lord, nor for the spiritual welfare of souls, but for its own advantage and temporal interests, it ought to force its affections towards the contrary, insisting on this in prayer and other spiritual exercises and imploring God to grant it a contrary mind, protesting that it does not wish for the said office or benefice, nor for anything else, unless His Divine Majesty, bringing its desires into order, so changes its first affection, that its only motive for desiring or possessing one thing or another may be the service, honour, and glory of His Divine Majesty.[10]

Although this state of indifference in man's own will is of decisive importance in elucidating the problem of Donne's response to Morton, we must be careful not to become confused about one matter. The state of indifference described above is by no means to be identified with total desirelessness. Thus "inordinate affections" must be carefully distinguished from the true "affections" of the soul. Such affections were to be actively promoted. After

9. *Ibid.*
10. *Ibid.,* p. 16.

all, right "desires" [11]—one's equivalent to God's will—were
the whole point of the prayer. "Indifference" meant equally
balanced feelings toward any two or more possible courses
of action. By balancing one desire against its opposite, the
performant got rid of "inordinate" affections. In each case
the desires to be balanced were consciously conceived. Only
when the choice was made according to a will arising from
some hidden source, some source not part of his conscious
will (now rendered temporarily impotent by this conscious
counterbalancing activity), was it presumed to be God's
will. That hidden source is what we would today call the
"subconscious." Thus, when he consciously chose what was
subconsciously presented to him, those two aspects of his
nature were joined—and it was precisely then that he
moved toward the goal God wanted for him; and for this
the preparation of "indifference" was essential. Indifference
was how the performant of the exercises assured himself
that he did not merely move toward some already con-
sciously conceived world pattern.[12]

Surely Donne refers to this aspect of the tradition of the
Spiritual Exercises when he associates with his "frequent"
efforts at "praier," "equal and indifferent affections" during
the years of "irresolutions" which preceded his writing
Pseudo-Martyr in 1610. The problem of conscience that
Donne's "best of casuists" had raised for him is formulated
in a way very close to the language of the passages I have
quoted from the *Spiritual Exercises*. Donne had said that

11. *Ibid.*, p. 69.
12. The assumption of this paragraph that the voice of God
emerges into man's life through the unconscious was drawn from
O. Hobart Mowrer's *The Crisis in Psychiatry and Religion*
(Princeton: Princeton University Press, 1961), especially the
chapter entitled "Changing Conceptions of the Unconscious,"
pp. 17–39. For example, on page 32 he summarizes his position
in saying that "religion, at its best, is always concerned with the
unconscious, conceived as conscience and the voice of God."

his guide agreed that in such decisions the soul's "only motive for desiring one thing or another [should] . . . be the . . . glory of His Divine Majesty." To be sure, it was allowed that a maintenance and God's glory could both be wanted, but in that case "God's glory should be the first end, and a maintenance the second motive to embrace that calling." Although the tone is clearly in the Ignatian tradition of spirituality, this wording more than anything else suggests that the *Spiritual Exercises* was not its specific origin. Donne's writer, with his hierarchical distinctions of first and second motives, sounds more Scholastic than Saint Ignatius, who furthermore would ordinarily not have been called a casuist.

But perhaps the most important thing to notice in this second reason given to Morton is that Donne's feeling is not determined by the rules which his guide has formulated to instruct his conscience. He does not state that he prefers the second motive to the first, or the first to the second, but only that he is puzzled. When he consults his conscience, he says, he feels "at this time so perplexed about it, that I can neither give myself nor you an answer." What happens to John Donne will be affected by the instructed conscience of his casuist, no doubt, and by other broad patterns of the period. But he is not, after all, going to repeat the life of Saint Ignatius, nor is he destined to become a Jesuit or even to receive the stamp of an inner life slavishly modeled on the *Spiritual Exercises*. The *Spiritual Exercises* did not indeed require that. It was the actual conscience of the person performing the exercises that counted. All the rest the performant was advised to become indifferent to.

If Donne felt perplexed in his conscience in the presence of such clear instructions, we may well suspect that he had been entertaining some other considerations which are not reported to us here. And that is exactly what we are told next: "To these," Walton shows Donne concluding, "I might add other reasons that dissuade me; but I crave your favour that I may forbear to express them, and thankfully decline your offer."

What were these unspoken reasons? Gosse thinks they were theological reservations. But this is unlikely. It was precisely in the area of theological study that Donne and Morton had previously worked together closely, and Morton must have decided to speak to Donne as he did on the basis of that previous relationship. Gosse's own characterization of Morton shows his courteous and sensitive manner even with forthright and stubborn recusants. Theology was the grand whipping boy for religious evangelicals of Gosse's generation, but we must look beyond such simple nineteenth- and early twentieth-century conventions about the nature of the religious life. They hang too much on the same dissociated psychology which for so long destroyed the reception of Donne's early verse. Since these additional reasons are not included in Walton's record, we must look elsewhere for the grounds which might disclose these motives.

I find the necessary clues in "A Litany," a poem Donne wrote probably in 1608 (or 1609). This was the period immediately following the encounter with Morton, a time when he must have been wrestling deeply with the problem of vocation. That "A Litany" grew out of his meditations in specific relation to concerns over the visible church is indicated by the letter describing it which he wrote to Sir Henry Goodyer. Donne there explained that its "devotion" was "rectified" in such a way as to require its derogation neither by "the Roman Church . . . nor the Reformed." [13]

13. Gosse, *Life,* I, 196. More fully, Donne says his poem "will deserve best acceptance . . . [in] that neither the Roman Church need call it defective, because it abhors not the particular mention of the blessed triumphers in heaven, nor the Reformed can discreetly accuse it of attributing more than a rectified devotion ought to do."

In a penetrating observation on Donne's "A Litany,"
Helen Gardner notes that its attitudes "contrast most inter-
estingly with . . . Senecan despising of the world." The
full context of her remarks on this point is worth quoting,
because it shows how the court symbolized the world, not
only for Donne but for the Jacobeans generally. She says
that Donne's

> declarations that happiness may exist in courts, and that the
> earth is not our prison . . . contrast most interestingly with
> the pessimism of some Jacobean writers, particularly Web-
> ster, with whom Donne is often compared. The dying
> Antonio's cry, "And let my Sonne, flie the Courts of
> Princes," and Vittoria's last words, "O happy they that
> never saw the Court," only sum up the constant Senecan
> despising of the world in Webster's two greatest plays. "A
> Litany" has none of this cynicism. It is . . . a singularly
> unbitter poem, although it was written at a bitter time.

The whole is summarized by her speaking of the poem's
"resolute rejection of otherworldliness." [14]
However, Miss Gardner finds it hard to reconcile world-
liness with her exclusively spiritual conception of what a
"religious" poem should be. Unlike the Holy Sonnets,
whose meditations are modeled on the tradition of mental
prayer and which therefore "give an immediate impression
of spontaneity," [15] the "inferior" "Litany" is "an elaborate
private prayer, rather incongruously cast into a liturgical
form," whose "incompatibility" with its subject she also
describes as "twisted to fit the material." [16] Such a "twisted"
reconciliation between the interior (the voice of the
psyche) and the exterior (the voice of the traditional

14. Helen Gardner, *The Divine Poems*, pp. xxvi–xxvii.
15. *Ibid.*, p. xxix.
16. *Ibid.*, p. xxviii.

church litany) is, of course, the mark of the mannerist stance.

Could Miss Gardner's failure to identify this poem as an expression of mannerism have led her to put a negative case upon its aesthetic character? In addition to comparing it unfavorably to the Holy Sonnets, she makes the improbable suggestion that Donne might have falsified his actual feelings of *contemptus mundi:* the poem "may reflect his need, at this time, to assure himself that the way that appears easier is not, for that reason, necessarily wrong," for, "the temptation to despise what one has not obtained and to cry, because one has been unsuccessful, 'the world's not worth my care' is strong to ambitious natures. It must have been strong to Donne." [17]

This interpretation of the poet's feelings is inconsistent with her "most interesting" discovery of the contrast between "A Litany" and "Senecan despising of the world." Her estimate that Donne must fundamentally feel "the world's not worth my care" probably goes back to her over-all aesthetic of religious poetry. She argues that religious poems are necessarily a minor species of poetry, agreeing with T. S. Eliot that they leave out "what men consider their major passions." [18] In Miss Gardner's handling, this aesthetic is clearly derivative from her fundamental notion of Christian "experience" as a set of tepid rationalizations. Compare her evaluation of "A Litany" with the over-all interpretation of Donne as a religious poet which she presents in her general introduction to the Divine Poems:

> [Donne] remains a wit in his divine as in his secular verse; but the "fierce endeavour" of his wit is tamed: the outra-

17. *Ibid.,* pp. xxv–xxvi.
18. *Ibid.,* p. xv, quoted from T. S. Eliot, "Religion and Literature," *Essays Ancient and Modern* (New York: Harcourt, Brace, 1936), p. 96.

geous element has disappeared. . . . The divine poet is to some degree committed to showing himself as he would be rather than as he is. . . . Donne, though in many other ways a remarkable human being, is not remarkable for any spiritual gifts and graces which we recognize at once as extraordinary and beyond the experience of the majority of mankind. For all his genius as a poet, his intellectual vivacity and his passionate and complex temperament, his religious experience seems, as with most of those who profess and call themselves Christians, to have been largely a matter of faith and moral effort.[19]

But the "fierce endeavour" of Donne's wit is not tamed in "A Litany." The "outrageous element" has not "disappeared." That is precisely the problem. When he should be rejecting the world, we discover him outrageously hanging onto it. Why should we think this poem shows nothing "remarkable" in "spiritual gifts and graces"? And why should we think it proceeds from some lukewarm and fundamentally hypocritical "faith and moral effort" which Miss Gardner believes to be characteristic of "most of those who profess and call themselves Christians"? Why must we believe that his "outrageous" attitude in a poem on women is authentic, but when it is on a religious theme he must only be "showing himself as he would be rather than as he is"? Although I believe Miss Gardner's aesthetic faulty, her Christian knowledge weak, and consequently her interpretation incorrect, the very difficulty she has in explaining the qualities she observes is a testimony to her accuracy in seeing. Donne's religion is not Miss Gardner's. It is not all spiritual and inner. It is worldly; and "A Litany," as shocking as it may be to modern mentality, is in fact both a religious and a worldly poem.

But the world it insists on is the *whole* world, not the half-a-world which modernity has tacitly agreed to under-

19. Gardner, *The Divine Poems,* pp. xvi–xvii.

stand by the term "worldly." Donne just as resolutely
rejects the exclusively unspiritual as he does the exclusively
unworldly, and that is why we find his religious poetry so
hard to receive. Thus, in the stanza which probably led
Miss Gardner to assert Donne's "resolute rejection of
'otherworldliness,' " he prays for his deliverance as follows:

> From being anxious, or secure,
> Dead clods of sadnesse, or light squibs of mirth,
> From thinking, that great courts immure
> All, or no happinesse, or that this earth
> Is only for our prison fram'd,
> Or that thou art covetous
> To them whom thou lov'st, or that they are maim'd
> From reaching this worlds sweet, who seek thee thus,
> With all their might, Good Lord deliver us.[20]

Here Donne requests of the Lord that those who "seek thee
thus," that is, deeply within the inner life, will not there-
fore be tempted to fall into hatred of the outer world. The
world he pleads for is similar to the world implied by the
Spiritual Exercises, where the spiritual man was certainly
not told that choosing something in the world was in itself
evil. The world was good. Evil choices were not even
contemplated. One was to pray only over things "good or
indifferent" in themselves. If one were to choose between
poverty and riches, for example, this was not to make a
choice between good and evil. Either choice, rightly made,
would be a good. "Senecan despising of the world" simply
had no place whatever in this prayer.

But in the *Spiritual Exercises* there was a confusing com-
plication: the need for "indifference" toward the choice one
was to make in the world, to be achieved by the principle
of balancing opposites. One was not to "wish for health

20. *Ibid.,* p. 21. Other quotes from "A Litany" in this chapter
are from the same source, pp. 16–26.

more than sickness, for wealth more than poverty, for
honour more than dishonour"; and, if one found one's soul
"inordinately" attached to some good thing, that is, too
much affected toward one thing only, one was "to force its
affections to the contrary." To be sure, the principle of
balance as expressed in the *Spiritual Exercises* would seem
to have been directed with a reverse emphasis to what is
found in "A Litany." In the *Spiritual Exercises* the man
who was tempted to seek worldly success and esteem was
admonished to counteract this by forcing his affections
toward sickness, poverty, or dishonor. Donne's poem, on
the whole, and this stanza in particular, changes the em-
phasis so as to force his affections toward the world. But
Donne was writing after having so successfully forced his
affections against the temptations described in the *Spiritual
Exercises* that he *actually* was living in poverty, and some
sickness too, and, if without dishonor, at least with not
much honor. This sense of otherworldliness—ridding him-
self of excessive attachment to the things of this world
while he yet remains connected to it—is quite clear in the
poem. Thus, addressing his petition to Christ, Donne says:

> Through thy submitting all, to blowes
> Thy face, thy clothes to spoile, thy fame to scorne,
>   All waies, which rage, or Justice knowes,
> And by which thou could'st shew, that thou wast born,
>   And through thy gallant humblenesse
>   Which thou in death did'st shew,
> Dying before thy soule they could expresse,
> Deliver us from death, by dying so,
> To this world, ere this world doe bid us goe.

To have arrived at the outcast state in which he was then
living was to Donne a spiritual achievement. Having
achieved it, however, it was now just as necessary not to
overvalue it.

"Dying to this world" was not without its pleasures. During this period Donne was living the life of a scholar and poet; he could see himself as a hero of the spiritual life, having spiritual grandeurs. But such pleasures are not without their dangers: overdoing the isolation, developing melancholia or despair. He needed—as always—to "force his affections to the contrary," and so he also prayed:

> When want, sent but to tame, doth warre
> And worke despaire a breach to enter in,
> . . . .
> When wee are mov'd to seeme religious
> Only to vent wit, Lord deliver us.

From side to side swing the attitudes of the poem. Whenever a danger of valuing one world at the expense of the other shows up, the poet moves to the contrary. Miss Gardner is right if by speaking of Donne's "resolute rejection of 'otherworldliness' " she meant his resolute rejection of "Senecan despising of the world," but not otherwise. For Donne's attitude was fundamentally Christian rather than Stoic. He affirmed this world *and* the other, and he rejected everything less paradoxical than that.

It is hard for many persons not genuinely familiar with the New Testament or Christian tradition to understand Christian worldliness. Part of Miss Gardner's difficulty probably results from her failure to distinguish between Stoic and Christian "despising of the world." The Christian attitude is never fundamentally antiworldly, nor is this the attitude described of God or of Jesus in the biblical tradition. Those who deny Christian worldliness overlook the commonplaces of almost every major branch of Christianity, ranging from those which emphasize the traditional orthodox doctrines of the incarnation (God born in the flesh) and the redemption (of the world) to the Protestant biblicists, who tirelessly quote John 3:16 ("For God so

loved the world that he gave his only Son") and even to
the recent so-called radicals of the secular gospel.[21] The
Christian sees this world, or the flesh which participates in
it, as an enemy as long as it is not redeemed by the entry of
the power of God. At a certain stage or under certain
conditions of life men are indeed victimized by this world.
In this state man is enslaved to the flesh; that is, he is domi-
nated by externals—by things which pass away. But man is
meant to be free, that is, to dominate those things. This can
happen only to the degree that the psyche permits itself to
be regenerated, or made potent, by the basic source of life,
historically termed, in the English language, "God." Saint
Paul expresses it this way: "Do not be conformed to this
world but be transformed by the renewal of your mind," as
the Revised Standard Version words it.[22] Or, as J. B. Phillips
renders it, "Don't let the world around you squeeze you
into its own mould, but let God re-mould your minds from
within." [23] "Let your minds be remade and your whole
nature thus transformed," says the *New English Bible*.[24]
Through the participation of his flesh in the world, the man
whose psyche receives that seminal power is then able to
participate in bringing the new world into being. Stoicism,
on the other hand, sees the world and the spirit in irreversi-
ble conflict and mutual hostility, so that the best one can
hope for in this world is either to be able to endure the
pain of it or to make oneself, somehow, passionless.[25]

21. For example, Paul M. Van Buren in his *The Secular
Meaning of the Gospel: Based on an Analysis of Its Language*
(New York: Macmillan, 1963).
22. Romans 12:2.
23. *Letters to Young Churches* (New York: Macmillan,
1950), p. 28.
24. (Oxford: Oxford University Press, 1961).
25. See the comment on Stoic apathy in Moses Hadas, ed. and
trans., *The Stoic Philosophy of Seneca: Essays and Letters of
Seneca* (New York: W. W. Norton, 1958), Introduction, p. 24.
See also Edwyn Bevan, "Lecture II," *Stoics and Sceptics* (Ox-
ford: Oxford University Press, 1913).

But isn't Donne's worldliness to be understood as Angli-
can rather than Christian? For if the Christianity of
Donne's time was fundamentally worldly and the court was
the symbol of the world, how was it that the Puritans
tended to reject the court? Weren't some major branches of
Christianity antiworldly? No. World-rejection was no more
fundamentally characteristic of the Puritans than of the
Anglicans or the Roman Catholics, nor did these groups
differ primarily in the degree of tension felt between the
inner life and the outer world. They were all both inner-
and outer-oriented. They differed principally in the symbols
in which they experienced the inner life and in the corre-
sponding structures in the external world into which they
poured their constructive psychic and bodily energies. Each
religious group had its own characteristic religio-political
vision and participated in the movement of the times by
centering this vision more and more in one particular
person or body. Thus the Roman Catholic saw an interna-
tional hierarchy centered in the pope, the Anglican saw a
national church-state centered in the king, and the Puritan
saw the chosen people of God centered in the parliament.
Each group also had a characteristic vision of the nature of
the "old world" now passing away, which presented to
them the threat of mere conformity. And it was this world,
the world that was passing away, that had to be rejected in
favor of the world that was coming to be. For Donne,
conformity meant conforming to an exclusive center in the
papacy, and the reconstructive psychic energy of his life
was poured into the "new world," focused on the king.

More will be said about the distinction between Stoic
and Christian attitudes in the next chapter, but here it is
enough if I have shown that world-negation in Christianity
is for the sake of world-affirmation. One side of this para-
dox cannot be held to exclude the other, as it can in
Stoicism. That Donne presents both attitudes toward the

world in "A Litany" is simply a form of ordinary Christian ambivalence. That he balances one against the other by bringing each into a directly visible contrast with the other, hiding the reconciliatory path between, represents his participation in the mannerist mode of that ambivalence.

So far my quotations have shown Donne rejecting either one or the other in separate passages. Let me conclude this discussion by giving in full the stanza last quoted above, where the two attitudes are intimately balanced. A set of antiworldly lines alternates with a succeeding set of anti*un*worldly lines, and so back and forth. The first couplet prays for deliverance from sensual temptation:

> When senses, which thy souldiers are,
> Wee arme against thee, and they fight for sinne,
> When want, sent but to tame, doth warre,
> And worke despaire a breach to enter in,
>   When plenty, Gods image, and seale
>   Makes us Idolatrous,
> And love it, not him, whom it should reveale,
> When wee are mov'd to seeme religious
> Only to vent wit, Lord deliver us.

Donne is just as afraid of the dangers of the inner life, if it should be pushed too exclusively, as he is of the outer life, and vice versa. The essential point is to have both, and to have both as deeply and fully and genuinely as possible within the experience of one man and one lifetime. That is Donne's form of Christian worldliness.

If we now add to this view another of Miss Gardner's observations on "A Litany," we shall be able to return with the clues needed to make a plausible guess at the character of Donne's undisclosed motives in rejecting Morton's offer. Miss Gardner points out that the long list of sins from which the poet requests deliverance ignores the traditional medieval classifications, the "sins against God and sins against my neighbour, or the seven deadly sins and their branches. Instead," she says, "the sins in 'A Litany' can all be referred back to two general philosophic conceptions: the conception of virtue as the mean between two extremes, and the related conception of virtue as the proper use of all the faculties." [26] This is true. (In passing, note that the awkward marriage of *philosophic* virtue to the decidedly *liturgical* form of "A Litany" is another instance of mannerist contortion.) But what is the character of these two philosophic virtues in themselves?

The second of them is related to the first; the proper use of man's faculties is the means by which the extremes are reconciled. But the extremes must first be revealed—or created—in order to be reconciled. And man needs to use all his faculties in this, first to bring the extremes into being and then to reconcile them. By hiding from this world, man is able successfully to contemplate it as empty of his own personal presence. Without himself, who is the only material object whose juncture with psychic reality he can experience from the inside out, he sees the world in two, in poles of self and other-than-self, which are the analogues of the other world and this world. However, he hides away not only to experience this separation but also to gain the power to overcome it. In his retreat he gathers that awareness of power within himself the more deeply, so as to be able finally to jump dramatically into the breach and hold

26. *The Divine Poems,* p. xxvii. Compare with Saint Thomas on the question of "Whether the Moral Virtues Consist in a Mean," in which the central problem is to reconcile two statements from Aristotle: "Virtue is the peak of power" and "Moral virtue is an elective habit consisting in the mean" (*Summa,* Question LXIV, quoted from *The Basic Writings of Saint Thomas Aquinas,* ed. Anton C. Pegis, 2 vols. [New York: Random House, 1945], II, 488). The whole passage is of such extraordinary relevance to Donne's art and to the course of his life that I have quoted a large part of it in an appendix, pp. 179–80, below.

things together before it is too late and the world irremedi-
ably and absolutely splits asunder. In his separating himself
from this world, both of them "die," and in his leap back
again into the world, he "creates" both anew.

In order for man to mediate the new world in the
mannerist style, he may not ultimately hold back from
participation, nor may he content himself with some mere
partial realization of his powers; he must first die to the
world, and then he must deliver himself into the world, all
of himself, psyche into body and both together into the
activity of reconciling the world polarities. This is a mag-
nificent vision of virtue. Perhaps no man can fully achieve
it; but if he has it and fails, he stands judged by that
failure, and in that case he can be justified only by some-
thing outside himself. He cannot deliberately and know-
ingly choose less.

But less is precisely what the help Morton offered would
have required Donne to accept. The key to this limitation
on the mannerist's magnificent virtue is specified in the
principal condition of the offer—clearly reported by Wal-
ton and implied, in any case, because the person from
whom it came was not the king: Morton asked Donne to
"waive your Court hopes, and enter into holy orders."
Donne would not waive his court hopes as a condition of
ordination in the church, not then or ever; for the court
was to Donne the symbol of the world.

Morton's requirement entailed a very specific conflict for
a Christian of Donne's particular world experience. He was
brought up in a Roman Catholic household surrounded by
a political community largely turning Anglican. The chief
grounds upon which the Anglican church had officially
broken with Roman Catholicism was over the respective
authorities of pope and king in England. Obedience to the
king had been the very point of the pamphlets which
Donne had assisted Morton to prepare; three years later it

was to be the point of Donne's own *Pseudo-Martyr.* To be sure, an Englishman could remain Roman Catholic if the realm of authority of pope and king could be separated, the one to be spiritual and the other temporal; and many English Catholics held this view. But an Anglican could not maintain this split. Indeed, to become an Anglican was precisely one of the modes by which it was repaired: the king was head of England *and* the church. So why, then, should a man turning Anglican from fundamentally Roman Catholic antecedents give up his court hopes in order to "enter into holy orders"? If he had no hope in the king as head of his church, why not remain Roman Catholic? Donne was to find the answer to the problem posed by the third Satire precisely here, in the king, the one man who *justly* claimed God's power.

Donne did have hope in his king, in spite of many difficulties—in the court, in himself, and in the temper of the times. He blindly and faithfully, foolishly and prudently, stubbornly and magnificently clung to the desire to obtain his preferment from that very court which Morton asked him to abandon. Furthermore, if Donne was to serve the church-state through the state church, he wanted what his mannerist ethic taught him to hope for: a magnificent fulfillment of all of his powers. Like the new style of relationship of authority discovered by the Jesuits, Donne wanted to skip over the old feudal intermediaries in the hierarchy and make his allegiance directly to the top.

If this view is correct, it resolves several puzzles. It would enable us to grasp in some convincing way why the casuistical logic that required Donne to hold the glory of God superior to his own maintenence left him perplexed and confused about his religious vocation. For this way of relating the religious to the worldly does not accord well with the mannerist attitude and moral temper growing more and more to be his own. The new style of joining polar opposites is no longer well expressed in such stepladder-like hierarchical distinctions as that between, first, "God's glory" and, second, "a maintenance." That was late medieval or early Renaissance. The new style called for understanding these as polarities and joining them by a leap, intuitively or in the dark, as it were, and not according to the more or less fully visible and rational models of relationship required by his "best of casuists."

Finally, the considerations brought forth here provide a suggestion for those "other reasons" which Donne begged Morton's "favour that I may forbear to express." It is hard to tell a man, even harder perhaps if the man is a friend, that you prefer to be helped by another greater than he or that you do not think his preferment of sufficient stature to engage all of your powers.

Or could it be that Donne did really reveal some of these considerations to Morton? What other clergyman, save possibly Dr. John King, the bishop of London, did he know as well or well enough to use him as his spiritual director? Perhaps he did discuss his ambitions with Morton more fully than the report from Walton indicates. In that case I think we may easily believe that Morton hid this kind of thinking from Walton. Morton and Donne were far closer to each other, personally, historically, religiously, than either of them was to Walton, and Donne might far more likely have trusted Morton with the intimate thoughts of his heart than Morton would have trusted them with a mind like Walton's.

CHAPTER V

THE DEPTHS

Though the encounter with Morton had left Donne no better off financially than before, he certainly had not been unaffected by it spiritually. One of the results was that, soon after Morton's proposal, Donne began to declare himself unmistakably an Anglican. To be sure, his affirmation of the Anglican position was not made publicly until 1610, when he took the risk (with those who would impugn his motives) of publishing *Pseudo-Martyr*. Mrs. Simpson, in commenting on this and the publication of *Ignatius his Conclave* the following year, concludes that their tone shows that Donne "was evidently by this time a convinced Anglican." [1] If private conviction is meant, however, we have the evidence of his personal correspondence to show that he was a "convinced Anglican" by 1608, the very year after Morton's offer. In two letters written to Sir Henry Goodyer, Donne refers to "our" church in a way

1. Evelyn M. Simpson, *A Study of the Prose Works of John Donne*, 2d ed. (Oxford: Oxford University Press, 1948), p. 27.

which makes his feeling for the Anglican church unmistakable, referring in one to "continence in the Roman Church, and order and decency in ours" and in the other to having heard from a visitor "that our Church hath lost Mr. Hugh Broughton, who is gone to the Roman side." [2]

To be sure, these letters cannot be exactly dated, but the first of them refers to "a letter in verse" which Donne owes his correspondent, and he paid this debt while he was living at Mitcham [3] between 1605 and 1608, which requires it to have been written prior to 1609. Gosse dates it, in brackets, "*July?* 1607," the very month after Morton's offer. The second letter refers to his composing "A Litany" and also to a "Book" which he had apparently just finished writing but which he never "purposed to print." This book must be *Biathanatos,* which, with other evidence, leads Miss Gardner to suggest dating the poem, and hence the letter also, in autumn, 1608.[4] This is about where Gosse placed it. Taken all together, the bits of evidence that these references to "our" church were written after the interview with Morton are convincing; that they were written before the publication of *Pseudo-Martyr* in 1610 seems to me certain.

Douglas Bush's assertion that Donne's position in 1597–98 as secretary to Sir Thomas Egerton shows that he "must have become by this time, if not by the time of the third 'Satire,' at least a nominal Anglican" [5] is inevitable if what Bush means by "nominal Anglican" is one who has taken the Oath of Obedience. Many practicing Roman

2. Gosse, *Life,* I, 170 and 196.
3. See the concluding lines of the verse letter to Sir Henry Goodyer in Herbert J. C. Grierson, *The Poems of John Donne,* 2 vols. (Oxford: Oxford University Press, 1912), I, 184.
4. Helen Gardner, *John Donne: The Divine Poems,* 2d ed. (Oxford: Oxford University Press, 1964), p. 81.
5. *English Literature in the Earlier Seventeenth Century: 1600–1660,* 2d ed. (Oxford: Oxford University Press, 1962), footnote, p. 133.

Catholics took the Oath, as Morton and Donne argued they should, and someone of Donne's uncertain religious position could certainly have taken it without injury to his conscience.[6] Morton's courtesy to known recusants shows that he could well have employed a sensitive and sympathetic "nominal Anglican" as his assistant, perhaps thinking even then that he might be able to move him further yet. It would seem that the stages of Donne's church affiliation were: Roman Catholic childhood, no church in early manhood (the third Satire), nominal Anglican in his mid- to late twenties (secretary to Sir Thomas), some kind of personal and private identity with the Anglican church in 1607–8 (evidence of the letters), convinced and professing Anglican by 1610 (publication of *Pseudo-Martyr*).

But the inner conditions with which Donne was grappling during this period were far more profound than anything which can be summarized in this way. For several reasons, one set openly expressed, the other hidden, he had felt he had to reject Morton's offer. If I have interpreted the hidden motives badly, the others make it clear enough that he did not yet feel satisfied with his inner life. He was not convinced that he had reached that state of balance toward the alternative conditions of the world which the *Spiritual Exercises* called indifference. And it was only when this state was reached that one could believe that the movements he felt in his soul truly were of God. Tempted, at least in a part of himself, no doubt, to overcome the poverty and irrelevance he felt in his life by accepting the mediate resolution offered by Morton, he chose a direction for his actual life contrary to that temptation. This was what the *Spiritual Exercises* had advised the soul to do:

6. See also Chapter 1, "The Letter of the Law," in Martin Havran, *The Catholics in Caroline England* (Stanford: Stanford University Press, 1962), for evidence of how Roman Catholics survived even in highly placed situations.

"Thus, if it be desirous to seek and possess some office or benefice, not for the honour and glory of God our Lord, nor for the spiritual welfare of souls, but for its own advantage and temporal interests, it ought to force its affections towards the contrary." [7] Donne forced his affections to the contrary, and instead of moving outwardly toward the polarity of the external world he turned toward the psychic pole, driving the gulf of separation between inner and outer all the deeper. Let us look at another passage in the *Spiritual Exercises* expressing the right state in which to make the choice of vocation. "The Preamble to making the Election" presents two possible vocations as examples, the one marriage, the other a benefice:

In every good Election, so far as regards our part, the eye of our intention ought to be single, looking only to the end for which I am created, viz. for the praise of God our Lord, and the salvation of my soul. Therefore whatever I choose ought to be for this, that it may help me towards the end for which I am created: not ordering or drawing the end to the means, but the means to the end. As, for example, it happens that many first choose to marry, which is a means, and in the second place to serve God our Lord in the married state, which service of God is the end. In the same way there are others who first desire to possess benefices, and then to serve God in them. So that these persons do not go straight to God, but rather wish that God should come straight over to their inordinate affections, and consequently they make of the end a means, and of the means an end, so that what they ought to choose first they choose last. For first we ought to make it our object to desire to serve God, which is the end; and secondarily to accept the benefice, or to marry (if that should be more fitting for me), which is the means to the end. Nothing therefore ought to move me to take such means, or to deprive myself

7. Loyola, *Spiritual Exercises,* p. 16.

of them, except only the service and praise of God our Lord, and the eternal salvation of my soul.[8]

But Donne had married already. He found himself in mid-life having made little of himself in his own eyes and was now determined to come to grips with what his life was for. The way he did so was to plunge deeply into the new style of inner life. The *Spiritual Exercises* contained specific advice for what one who found himself in Donne's irresolute condition was to do.

This advice is contained in the "Second Method for making a sound and good Election." It consisted of four rules, two of which are closely related to the themes of Donne's writing, love and death, during the next few years. These two are to propose to oneself

> that the love which moves me and makes me choose the said thing, should descend from on high, from the love of God: in such a manner that he who chooses should first feel in himself that the love which he has more or less for the thing which he chooses is solely for the sake of his Creator and Lord,

and

> to consider, as if I were at the point of death, the form and measure which I should then desire to have observed in the method of the present Election; and regulating myself according to that, let me make my decision on the whole matter.[9]

Though there is little evidence to separate the one of these themes from the other in the order of Donne's life, I shall begin by treating them separately, and the latter one first. I shall be able to treat this one more briefly because the story, in many important respects, has been thoroughly told in

8. *Ibid.*, p. 125.
9. *Ibid.*, p. 132.

Donald Ramsay Roberts' article "The Death Wish of John Donne." [10] Although I differ with Roberts in some perspectives, my principal task here is to articulate Donne's preoccupation with death, during this limited period of time only, into the over-all pattern of his life movement insofar as I am able to portray that in this study.

The common assumption, derived probably from Gosse,[11] that his experiences during this time were largely intellectual has this much truth in it—that they never excluded reason or "wit"; but they were certainly never composed of these alone. Largely out of touch with what he regarded as the meaningful world, Donne sank into a private and inner realm in which depression and excitement, combined with study and writing, deepened his understanding of the meaning of existence and also provided the means by which he was gradually and finally to bring those depths into contiguity with the external world. He knew what he wanted in some approximate kind of way: he wanted a vocation. And he knew from what quarter of

10. Donald Ramsay Roberts, "The Death Wish of John Donne," *PMLA,* LXII (1947), 958–76.
11. See Chapter VIII, "Controversial Works—Divine Poems," in Gosse, *Life,* I, esp. pp. 245 and 250. Other persons besides myself are aware of this error. For example, Evelyn Hardy, calling attention to Gosse's statement (*Life,* I, 161), "When he halts, when he plunges, it is the brain which steers him," says, "One of his biographers has described him as a man whose crises were always intellectual, but this is only partial truth. Donne was highly emotional as well as intellectual: the intellect, complex, original and strong, strove to control the emotions, which were in turn tormented by the intellect. The endearing simplicity of one half of his nature (and his conscientious consideration of the good Bishop's offer sprang from this source) was antagonistic to the self-condemnatory pride of the other, with which it was doomed forever to live. The balance of the nature swings violently from joy to dejection, from passion to recrimination, from action to melancholy pensiveness, and the vital force which drives him forward is blocked by that which is hostile to life itself" (*Donne: A Spirit in Conflict* [London: Constable, 1942], p. 108).

the world he wanted it to come. One practical problem
stood in the way. Any vocation originating from the court
would have required that he be close enough to make this
call likely, but in 1608 and 1609 Donne was in retreat at
his "hospital at Mitcham," in possession of neither the
money nor the friends necessary to bring him to notice.
Three or four years later, when his position was somewhat
improved, he still complained that he had not the "fortune"
which "would afford me any room" in the "world." He
presents his vocationless situation in that letter under the
metaphor of death: "I died ten years ago," he says, speaking
of his dismissal from Egerton's service following his mar-
riage in late 1601. The whole passage is worth quoting. His
correspondent is Sir Henry Wotton, then on a visit to
England from his embassage to The Hague:

> I learn that there is truth and firmness and an earnestness of
> doing good alive in the world; and therefore, since there is
> so good company in it, I have not so much desire to go out
> of it as I had if my fortune would afford me any room in it.
> You know I have been no coward, nor unindustrious in
> attempting that; nor will I give it over yet. If at last I must
> confess that I died ten years ago, yet as the Primitive
> Church admitted some of the Jews' ceremonies, not for
> perpetual use, but because they would bury the synagogue
> honourably, though I died at a blow then when my courses
> were diverted, yet it will please me a little to have had a
> long funeral, and to have kept myself so long above ground
> without putrefaction. But this is melancholic discourse.
>
> To change, therefore, from this metaphorical death to
> the true, and that with a little more relish of mirth, let me
> tell you. . . .[12]

With this letter, in which death is clearly linked to the
absence of vocation, the subject of Donne's so-called mor-
bidity is best introduced. Yet we cannot understand it if we

12. Gosse, *Life,* I, 291–92.

approach it only in modern contexts of meaning. "Death" meant for Donne, as for his contemporaries generally, the separation of body from soul (psyche, life),[13] and anything suggestive of that state was appropriately alluded to by that term. It is close to what Saint Paul means by the death of "the old man" and is a prelude to the experience of second birth. In this sense, it is a spiritual or psychic death and is felt as part of the totality of this life. The idea of death-in-life was a religious commonplace in Donne's time as familiar as its antithesis of life-in-death.[14]

The function of such a death is that the psyche, by becoming detached in some sense or other from the body and the whole of this world, may become more sensitive to the "other world" at whose door it lurks. The psyche wonders whether to escape there totally—in which case, however, joining the world becomes impossible. The only genuine promise lies in the hope that that experience will bring back with it something from the other side, giving to this world the element it needs to draw it toward its wholeness and to make, also, the person who is its agent a part of that wholeness. But the return—in the mannerist style of experience at any rate—is possible only for the soul which has previously moved off into what I have called the isolated cultivation of the inner life, which is the separation of soul and body constituting "death."

This death can be justified only if it is ultimately to be used for this world, not if it leads exclusively to the other one. Thus, in an important letter to Goodyer which Gosse dates in 1608, Donne writes of his suspiciousness of his

13. For one source of this concept see Saint Augustine, *The City of God* XIII. ii, "Of that Death which can Affect an Immortal Soul, and of that to which the Body is Subject" (*Basic Writings of Saint Augustine,* ed. Whitney J. Oates [New York: Random House, 1948], II, 210–11).

14. *The City of God* XIII. x, "Of the Life of Mortals, which is rather to be Called Death than Life" (Oates, II, 217).

own overearnest "desire of the next life." He knows that this feeling is "not merely out of a weariness of this," because he had the same feelings earlier in his life when he "enjoyed fairer hopes than now." In this state he seems to be "nothing," and this nothingness is identical to being without a vocation:

> But to be no part of any body is to be nothing. At most, the greatest persons are but great wens and excrescences; men of wit and delightful conversation but as moles for ornament, except they be so incorporated into the body of the world that they contribute something to the sustentation of the whole.[15]

Here Donne's desire for the "next life" is simultaneous with his desire to be "part of the world," showing that the mode of his inner life contains within it a decisive commitment to worldliness, a kind of worldliness which joined one's apprehensions of the other world to this one.

Donne, of course, is dissatisfied because he has not achieved this joining. He writes Goodyer:

> Because I am in a place and season where I see everything bud forth, I must do so too, and vent some of my meditations to you; the rather because all other buds being yet without taste or virtue, my letters may be like them. The pleasantness of the season displeases me. Everything refreshes, and I wither, and I grow older and not better, my strength diminishes, and my load grows.[16]

T. S. Eliot was not the first man to find that April is the cruelest month. Is Donne not describing the feeling more recently termed "alienation," which also is understood as a sense of being apart, a sense that, until one has joined the

---

15. Gosse, *Life,* I, 191.
16. *Ibid.,* p. 185.

world, one has not yet come into existence? "I would fain do something, but that I cannot tell what is no wonder. For to choose is to do; but to be no part of any body is to be nothing." [17]

Paralysis of the will as one form of the sense of separation from the world has been described by many men besides John Donne. It seems to come as a necessary stage in making an important decision. The stage of alienation, or "failing to choose," is "death"; it is, of course, death experienced in the midst of life. But it may itself be arrived at by means of a choice. Donne's rejection of Morton's offer placed him in the sharpest position of alienation that he ever experienced. The rebirth experience which follows when the sought-for decision is made likewise involves a paradox. Among the possibilities which face one, something must be chosen to become actualized, and something must be rejected, so that the choice requires a simultaneous affirmation and negation. These are the familiar paradoxes of actual experience: death and life, choosing and not choosing, affirmation and negation. They are not merely paradoxes of language, though language may of course express them; and expressing them may enter into their making. So in fact it was in this period of Donne's life. While he continued to choose death rather than make the premature assault upon the hill of truth which accepting Morton's offer would have required of him, he was engaged upon intense activity as a writer; and this was the means by which the link between the depths of the inner life and the external world was maintained.

Some of the results of this are embodied in his three early prose works: *Biathanatos,* written probably in 1608; *Pseudo-Martyr,* entered on the Stationers' *Register* for December 2, 1609; [18] and *Ignatius, his Conclave,* published in

17. *Ibid.,* p. 191.
18. Simpson, *The Prose Works of John Donne,* p. 159.

1611. Although these books are certainly learned and intellectual, they cannot rightly be looked upon as the mere rational exercises which the term "theology" has generally suggested to modernity and thus as detached from Donne's deeper psychic experiences.

Donne's explanation for writing *Biathanatos* shows that his descent into the inner life was so profound that the connection to the outer life was threatened with final separation:

> Beza . . . confesseth of himself, that only for the anguish of a Scurffe, which over-ranne his head, he had once drown'd himselfe from the Millers bridge in *Paris,* if his Uncle by chance had not then come that way; I have often such a sickely inclination. And, whether it be, because I had my first breeding and conversation with men of a suppressed and afflicted Religion, accustomed to the despite of death, and hungry of an imagin'd Martyrdome; or . . . [here Donne lists other reasons], mee thinks I have the keyes of my prison in mine owne hand, and no remedy presents it selfe so soone to my heart, as mine own sword.[19]

He goes on to argue in *Biathanatos* that some form of self-slaughter is possible and legitimate, citing Samson and others as instances. These examples show the act to be heroic and the person a martyr.

As Evelyn Simpson has noticed, the arguments of *Biathanatos* and *Pseudo-Martyr* are

> complementary, and the idea of self-inflicted death forms the link. In *Biathanatos* Donne argues that the general prohibition, *Thou shalt not kill,* covers the case of self-murder, and condemns it in general, but he dwells particularly on the point that this general law admits of certain excep-

19. *John Donne: "Biathanatos,"* reproduced from the 1st ed., with a bibliographical note by J. William Hebel (New York: Facsimile Text Society, 1930), pp. 17–18.

tions. . . . In all such cases it must be the motive and the attendant circumstances, not the bare act, argues Donne, by which our praise or condemnation is determined. In *Pseudo-Martyr* he lays stress on the other side of the argument. The Jesuits are urging the English Roman Catholics to refuse their allegiance to the king, on the ground that he is a heretic and has been dethroned by the Pope. They promise their followers a martyr's crown if insubordination is punished with death by the civil power. Donne argues that such a death is not martyrdom but suicide.[20]

Biathanatos is far more important for understanding the question of Donne's sincerity in becoming an Anglican than is commonly noticed. *Pseudo-Martyr* is the visible document which he used to justify his move. But *Biathanatos,* which he never published, is the invisible undergirding of the later work. For if Donne did not believe martyrdom a genuine and honorable possibility, what could be made of the argument of *Pseudo-Martyr?* *Biathanatos* shows that he did believe a man might rightly die for true religion. The truly worldly man will not only live for the world, but he will die for it as well. And Donne himself faced that possibility at a profound psychic level, when many things in his life might have tempted him to take the choice of self-slaughter, not the least of which was the anxiety attendant upon making any choice with confidence in a confused world situation. The important choices in Donne's life did not seem to him the mere affirmation of good over evil. They seemed rather to be choices among goods. He did not become an Anglican, for example, because he felt that medieval Christendom was wicked or even that Roman Catholicism was. Neither does death seem to Donne to be an evil choice. The problem of choosing between life and death is deeper than that. In speaking of the subtle wiles of the devil in connection with his longing for death, he came to grips with this moral problem. He is writing his closest friend, Goodyer:

> Two of the most precious things which God hath afforded us here, for the agony and exercise of our sense and spirit, which are a thirst and inhiation after the next life, and a frequency of prayer and meditation in this, are often envenomed and putrified, and stray into a corrupt disease; for as God doth thus occasion, and positively concur to evil, that when a man is purposed to do a great sin, God infuses some good thoughts which make him choose a less sin, or leave out some circumstance which aggravated that; so the devil doth not only suffer but provoke us to some things naturally good, upon condition that we shall omit some other more necessary and more obligatory. And this is his greatest subtlety, because herein we have the deceitful comfort of having done well, and can very hardly spy our error because it is but an insensible omission and no accusing act. With the first of these I have often suspected myself to be overtaken, which is with a desire of the next life; which though I know it is not merely out of a weariness of this, because I had the same desires when I went with the tide, and enjoyed fairer hopes than now; yet I doubt [i.e., suspect] worldly encumbrances have increased it.[21]

It is a good thing to thirst after the next life, but the devil may tempt us to choose a good thing at the expense of a better; here, he tempts Donne to choose the next life only —at the expense of living in this world also.

The Christian may rightly choose death for the sake of the Lord, and therefore for the sake of the world, but the grave problems of living never justified the Christian's dying for hate of the world or indifferent to it. Certainly a Christian might not die merely to escape the suffering he

---

21. Gosse, *Life,* I, 190–91. The bracketed interpolation is mine.

has in the world—a key point in Senecan Stoicism, as Moses Hadas explains: "A man must keep his soul free, and cleaving to reason will help him to do so; but when he has done all that a man can do for the ideal, when his pains are intolerable and hopeless, the door is always open and he is invited to step out of life." [22] Although Stoic attitudes are the very form and substance of modern "polite" or "respectable" Christianity, with its great concern that no perturbations or disturbances afflict life, yet it is clear enough that the over-all direction of Christian tradition is against it. Christian "suicide" rests fundamentally upon the figure of the suffering and death of Jesus understood as an example of God's action *for* the world. It is not based upon the vision of Seneca as a Stoic hero, taking poison at Nero's behest [23] and thus choosing death rather than suffering what the world might otherwise offer him. Although Donne's vision in *Biathanatos* seems at times to reflect something of the Stoic spirit, it is clearly founded more fundamentally upon the Christian view than upon the Stoic one.

Well aware of the charge of heresy that *Biathanatos,* if it were published, would draw against him, Donne was equally aware of the cry of coward which *Pseudo-Martyr* would raise. In publishing *Pseudo-Martyr* he did permit himself some public defense:

And for my selfe (because I have already received some light, that some of the Romane profession, having onely seene the Heads and Grounds handled in this Booke, have traduced me, as an impious and profane under-valewer of

22. Moses Hadas, ed. and trans., *The Stoic Philosophy of Seneca: Essays and Letters of Seneca* (New York: W. W. Norton, 1958), Introduction, p. 24. See also the description of Seneca's own suicide, pp. 7–8, and the conclusion to his letter "Suicide."
23. *Ibid.,* pp. 7–8.

Martyrdome), I most humbly beseech him, (till the read-
ing of the Booke, may guide his Reason) to beleeve, that I
have a just and Christianly estimation, and reverence, of
that devout and acceptable Sacrifice of our lifes, for the
glory of our blessed Saviour. For, as my fortune hath never
beene so flattering nor abundant, as should make this
present life sweet and precious to me, as I am a Moral man:
so, as I am a Christian I have beene ever kept awake in a
meditation of Martyrdome, by being derived from such a
stocke and race, as, I beleeve, no family, (which is not of
farre larger extent, and greater branches,) hath endured
and suffered more in their persons and fortunes, for obey-
ing the Teachers of Romane Doctrine, then it hath done. I
did not therefore enter into this, as a carnall or over-indul-
gent favourer of this life, but out of such reasons, as may
arise to his knowledge, who shall be pleased to read the
whole worke.[24]

Those who charge Donne with morbidity because of his
preoccupation with death and his longing for the next life
cannot also charge him with insincerity in having become
an Anglican. What such persons have to decide is the same
question that faced Donne: whether adherence to the pope
as the specific and decisive test of Christian faith, in an
England in which this meant the choice of actual death,
would have been martyrdom in fact, as the pope declared,
or merely suicidal, as Donne came to believe. My own
judgment is that he should be charged neither with insin-
cerity nor with "morbidity" in the usual modern under-
standing of the meaning of this word. In the psychological
terms in which such matters are discussed today, the issue
of "morbidity" revolves around how one grasps the mean-
ing of the death wish. Must it inevitably be taken as a sign
of sickness, or may it sometimes, or in some ways, be

24. From "Advertisement to the Reader," *Pseudo-Martyr*,
quoted from Simpson, *The Prose Works of John Donne*, pp.
183–84.

understood as an aspect of health? If the death wish as well
as the life wish is found in all persons, as it seems to be,
the problem is not whether it is wrong in itself but under
what circumstances or for what motive does it function
rightly? May the possibility of suicide never properly enter
a person's head, when the result is to drive him to grasp
more deeply what he may yet live his life for? Or indeed
what he might rightly be willing to die for? These are the
ways it functioned in Donne's life. The possibility of suicide
did enter his head, in many, many of its forms, subtle as
well as obvious; and that it might well be justified under
some conditions was an opinion he entertained abundantly.
It did drive him to consider what he was, and was not,
willing to die for. He was not willing to die to escape his
discomforts, and he was not willing to die for that form of
Christendom which, under the pressure of historical cir-
cumstances, had now become radically papal. And it did
drive him to consider that he might be willing to live for
the Anglican form of Christendom. The form of Christen-
dom and the discomfort were of course related, and the
choice of the Anglican form meant the hope also of escap-
ing from discomfort so severe that death might seem a
welcome release; but it also meant choosing life rather
than death as the means of escape.

Roberts believes that Donne's death wish was uncon-
scious and that he was afflicted with it because of his
childhood association with the Jesuits:

> The period of Donne's boyhood—let us say about
> 1580—is precisely the period when there were many por-
> tents of the ultimate failure of the Roman cause in Eng-
> land; when consequently the Jesuits in their attempt to
> effect a counter-reformation had reached their most desper-
> ate, intransigent, and fanatical state of mind. We may
> count John Donne as in some degree an innocent victim of
> this historical struggle. The apparent contradiction in the

suggestion that Donne was psychically infected by Jesuit fanaticism (or what he indubitably regarded as such) while at the same time he consciously rejected the cause and purposes of the Jesuits, is not a real one. The conscious and unconscious minds can readily take divergent paths.[25]

In some such way Donne's preoccupation with death led him to *Pseudo-Martyr*. In that book he declared that the position of the new Roman Catholicism, insofar as it rested in loyalty to the pope alone, was not worth dying for. In another country, or in another time, or to another person, to have chosen it would not have meant affirming the wish to die. But to Donne, in England, at this time, it seemed to do so.

Donne's decision was not a simple event. As Roberts rightly sees, it was simultaneously external and internal. At the same time that it rejected the ecclesiastical aspect of the new Jesuitical Catholicism, it also meant the rejection of what—in the light of that decision—appeared to be a suicidal form of the death wish. But Donne does accept something very like the specific form of the Jesuitical spiritual life, and he does accept the new mannerist life style, of which the Jesuits also represented a variant. Indeed, the extremist style of Jesuitical Catholicism, with its polarized spiritual and ecclesiastical commitments, made it all the easier for Donne to affirm the inner and deny the outer. Donne's decision was typically modern also in that he chose a national rather than an international religion. But in many respects, and in these the most important ones from the perspective of this study, Donne's decision was conservative and medieval: it allowed him to affirm a basic religious view which was simultaneously this- and other-worldly, political and ecclesiastical, secular and sacred. And if these same things could be said of the English Puritans,

25. Roberts, "The Death Wish of John Donne," p. 973.

Donne's choice in the external side of each of these duali-
ties supported the king and the court, and that was the old,
not the new, way. Furthermore, in choosing his models for
the imagery in which the inner life might be experienced,
he was also anti-Puritan, but not particularly so in making
use of the images of death and the other matters which
have been the concern of this chapter. He showed his
medieval, antimodern, and anti-Puritan side by being will-
ing also to admit into the spiritual life the matters I have
set aside for later, separate consideration, the images of
love, sex, and marriage. What Donne and his contemporar-
ies knew as the forms of the spiritual life we know, of
course, as psychology and myth.

CHAPTER VI

THE PSYCHIC
MARRIAGE

The sexual and marital imagery in Donne's "religious"
poems, taken all together, make up a myth of the
divine-human relationship in which each of the various
figures is a persona, or mask, of some aspect of Donne's
own—and man's—personal existence in the world.[1] It may
help the reader if, instead of building up an account of that
myth, step by step, with the bricks and mortar provided by
an elaborate apparatus of analysis of this poem and that, I
begin rather with the end product and then later show the
pertinent aspects of the story in their original locations in
the poems.

1. For an indication of the way in which traditional (includ-
ing Christian) myths may express personal and collective human
psychology see the excerpts from Jung's *The Relation between
the Ego and the Unconscious,* in *The Basic Writings of C. G.
Jung,* edited, with an introduction, by Violet Staub de Laszlo,
Modern Library edition (New York: Random House, 1959),
pp. 105–82.

Told as a more or less coherent and independent myth-narrative, the bare bones of the story are brief: it tells of the barren relations of body and soul in man's fallen existence, proceeds through a divorce, a new marriage—this time to the Lord—which results in the birth of a son, who now makes possible a fruitful and proper relationship of the body and soul. But this is too simple a version to be very helpful. I must provide a somewhat enriched account, which I shall do by dramatizing it and telling various parts in alternative terms, especially as I infer these from Donne's poems. The story is chiefly taken from the poems of the period 1608–11, some of which I shall inspect in the balance of this chapter, and even more importantly from the detached and controversial sonnet "Show me deare Christ, thy spouse, so bright and cleare," which I shall intepret extensively in the final chapter. My inferences throughout are extended by assimilation of Donne's language to significant sources of the over-all tradition of Christian humanism. Although I shall not cite these sources, most of them will be readily enough recognized by persons familiar with the classical and theological literature of the Renaissance-Reformation period. For example, I generally represent man's soul under the classical (and feminine) name "Psyche," and divine power under the Judaeo-Christian (and male) name "Lord"; in doing this, I am also trying to treat them in a personal language. But I shall describe these and other figures under various synonyms also, in an effort to connect the story with several philosophical, psychological, historical, and religious sources; without some of these connections the bare mythic persona will vanish into a meaningless emptiness. If some tension develops between various sets of dualities in my account, so much the better—the story is then closer to the mannerist paradigm.

Let me begin in a somewhat less personal style. The

more personal and less personal forms of the story, and the dual figures found in it, are, after all, analogous to one another. The body-psyche duality is analogous to the devil-God duality, and each of these is analogous to a this- and otherworldly duality. And each analogy is a mode of representing the participation of one duality in the other.

Under certain conditions, or at certain stages of life, the relationship between the body and the psyche is felt to be perverted, unnatural, or wrong. In the myth-narrative of the psychic marriage, this appears to be the result of an improper direction of domination. When the spirit is dominated by the flesh, the relationship is felt to be improper; and this is expressed mythically by saying that one is under the domination of the "world, the flesh, and the devil" or, more simply, that one is married to Satan. This enslaved condition is broken by God's marriage to man. As a result of the marriage, the otherworldly, or spiritual, polarity plays the dominant relationship to the this-worldly, material, or fleshly polarity. Hence, as a result of the marriage, we may say that God dominates the "world, the flesh, and the devil," replacing the perverted relationship represented by the earlier alternative. But let me now switch to a more personal, narrative, and dramatic form of telling the story.

Psyche, finding herself wrongly subjected to domination by the devil, a slavery to which she seems born, struggles to free herself in order to marry her true lover. Before this true marriage can be achieved, she must "divorce" herself from the world. i.e., she must escape its domination, a relationship in which the devil appears to be her "Lord," albeit her false Lord. Aware, however, that the condition of separation from the power of the flesh will feel so like death that she will feel threatened with total extinction, poor Psyche is afraid to undertake this step. Overcoming her reluctance, however, whether by decision, chance, fate, or divine intervention, she makes the separation; and alas, the reality does indeed support her fears. So accustomed has she been to giving in to the demands of the flesh that she is frightened almost out of her wits by the experience of her own powers. Having played the passive feminine role to what seemed to her to be the superior masculine initiative and energy of the flesh, she now feels herself totally without power or guidance and wanders about, lost and alone. All she seems able to do is to bewail the lack of a lover. She is now aware that the flesh is fundamentally impotent and that there is no use in going back, but she is tempted to believe that her true lover from the other world does not actually exist and that the only possibility for fulfillment is with that very devil whom she has just divorced. However, she does not give in to this despair. She is strengthened by some stories of mysterious origin which she has heard from her former husband, whom for that reason she cannot fully despise or reject. The dissatisfaction with this former marriage, together with the vague longings for the unknown "other," causes her to continue her search. At length, the unbelievable and inexpressible does happen; her importunity and complaints of emptiness are rewarded; her sorrows and rebuffs are turned to joy; she is joined to God, her true mate and true Lord.

In the consummation of this marriage something peculiar happens to her. Her supposed "feminine" nature is at first modified and is later reversed. The marital union of Psyche and her true Lord first produces a male-female person, "one neutrall thing," as Donne described sexual union in "The Canonization." [2] And when this union results in the birth of the divine-human son, the Christ

2. Herbert J. C. Grierson, *The Poems of John Donne,* 2 vols. (Oxford: Oxford University Press, 1912), I, 15.

(King or Ruler) of the Christian story, he is now discovered to be at the heart of the man's psychic life; the newborn child is Psyche herself, reborn. But in Psyche's rebirth, she is discovered this time in a male persona rather than a female one. As a result of this sexual transformation, Psyche, now "he," Saint Paul's "Christ who lives in me" (Gal. 2:20, RSV), is able to establish a new relationship to what formerly appeared to be the dominating world, flesh, and devil. Where Psyche had been nearly helpless in the face of the demands of her this-worldly "lord," now, through the union with the true Lord, "she" has now become the "he" to the "world, the flesh, and the devil," and these "material" structures must play the woman's role to the power of the "spiritual" King-husband within.

This role-reversal, or we may call it a persona-reversal, is not an impropriety for man's soul; it is rather a realization of its true state, since the soul was implanted in man to be his seminal and generative center. It was the earlier feminine persona that was a perversion due to the arrogance of the flesh, whose right function was merely to be the helpmeet to the soul. It is the psyche which should rightly penetrate the body, give form and movement to it, just as the larger analogous whole of which it is a part, the *anima mundi,* rightly gives form and movement to the material structure to which it is always to some degree joined. The psyche should do this both in fact and in the persona appropriate to this more dynamic and powerful reality, namely, in the male persona. The drama of this achievement is symbolized in the personae of the partners in the psychic marriage and in the subsequent son, who is the mask of the regenerated soul.

Although the marriage is primarily psychic, it implicates the material world. In the aftermath of the event, the regenerated soul has the authority to play the dominant role with its own body, and through that domination it can also add to the powers working in those several other dualities in which it participates, whose mutual participation is expressed in the various spiritual-material analogues. The regenerated psyche may now assist God in restoring the external world to its proper relationship to him. Insofar as this story has a root in Christian history, it is the biblical story of the historic event; and this story, in turn, is the seed by which the soul is reborn, so that there is no doubt but that the psychic marriage is achieved only with some mediation by the material world. One of the functions of the man with a regenerated soul is to pass on the seed. This is one way in which his new spiritual energy, through the now-submissive flesh, rightly penetrates the world. It is the Christian form by which the reborn psyche gives the world its enlivening spirit and fulfills its role as God's agent in the world. By means of the historical story, both in receiving and recreating it, then, the psyche is able to recapitulate Christ's action, and in this sense—the psyche's reception and subsequent proclamation of the story—God is continually and eternally reborn in union with the world. Thus, God himself (in the person of his son) dies (in the external, historical world) and rises again (in the reborn Christ-persona of the psyche of later man) in order to give the world its life.

In telling this story I have made no effort to distinguish the separate roles of the conscious and unconscious aspects of the psyche. Had I done so, the story would be subject to an almost infinite series of complications. The conscious and the unconscious each can play roles analogous to the male-female duality, and each may appear in the form of persona-reversal. The reversal will sometimes, as in the story as I told it, be apprehended as proper, sometimes as improper. Furthermore, the conscious and the unconscious can each be subdivided into new dualities; for example, each can be subdivided into an aspect of will and reason, so we can have a conscious will and an unconscious will, and we can have a conscious reason and an unconscious reason. And, in addition to these, it would easily be possible to discover a submerged third to go along with each duality, which would function as the dislocated mediating principle between the pairs of opposites struggling for domination. But except to suggest them here, to add such a series of complications to the story would only lead to hopeless confusions. I have told the story, I hope, with enough of its content and complexity to assist the interpretation of the poems; some of the complexities and subtleties will be shown or hinted at in the discussions to follow.

Now, how are the various parts of the story represented in the poems? I begin with the Divine Meditations, which, as Helen Gardner has shown, are almost certainly from the period 1608–11, and I discuss only those which are, or seem to be, concerned with the love of God. In these poems the soul, to some degree detached from this-worldly concerns but not in full possession of her freedom from the devil, wanders about on the brink of the other world, near despair, but hoping somehow to receive God's love. The situation is presented in the first sonnet:

> As due by many titles I resigne
> My selfe to thee, O God, first I was made
> By thee, and for thee, and when I was decay'd
> Thy blood bought that, the which before was thine,
> I am thy sonne, made with thy selfe to shine,
> Thy servant, whose paines thou hast still repaid,
> Thy sheepe, thine Image, and till I betray'd
> My selfe, a temple of thy Spirit divine;
> Why doth the devill then usurpe in mee?
> Why doth he steale, nay ravish that's thy right?
> Except thou rise and for thine owne worke fight,
> Oh I shall soone despaire, when I doe see

That thou lov'st mankind well, yet wilt'not [3] chuse me,
And Satan hates mee, yet is loth to lose mee.[4]

The octet shows the speaker's effort to join himself to God. He has placed himself into the relationship which the traditional titles due to God indicate. God is his Maker, Redeemer, Father, Master, Shepherd, and Spirit. At the beginning of the sestet he questions God: Why then is the devil able to do as he pleases? He declares that unless God will take the initiative, he will be lost. The concluding couplet drives at the heart of this poem and of several others of the Divine Meditations also; it indicates that the difference between God's love and Satan's hate is that Satan seems to clutch him while God stands by, hands off. The speaker wonders why his conscious efforts at humility described in the first eight lines are not enough to reward him with God's love, and he fails to see (or at least to say) how his own resentment works underground to stop off that very love.

In this poem the speaker seems to some degree to discover the unconscious in the persona of the devil. "Even though I (the consciousness) have submitted to God," the speaker seems to say, "the devil (the unconscious) has stolen me away." But that he finds this devil to be the persona for the unconscious is the sign that he is still in an

3. "The use, by Donne, of the apostrophe with no letter omitted is probably intended to indicate a speeding up in pronunciation without a complete elision" ("Notes to Donne," *Poetry of the English Renaissance, 1509–1660*, ed. J. William Hebel and and Hoyt H. Hudson [New York: F. S. Crofts, 1946], p. 987).

4. Helen Gardner, *John Donne: The Divine Poems,* from corrected sheets of the 1st ed. (Oxford: Oxford University Press, 1964), p. 6. The other quotations from Donne's Holy Sonnets: Divine Meditations in this chapter are from the same source, pp. 6–12. I have also referred to Helen Gardner's numbering of the sonnets.

improper relationship to himself. When the psychic marriage takes place, the conscious and unconscious will join, with the more hidden and invisible aspect of the psyche taking dominance over the more obvious and visible one, a dominance which will be acknowledged by the consciousness, in a loving surrender of its independent identity. And this will be simultaneous with a new joining of psyche and body, with the body acknowledging the psyche's dominance and similarly surrendering its independent identity. Likewise, when the marriage is ready to occur, the unconscious will appear in a divine persona, i.e., in the form of one who loves the consciousness, not in a demonic persona, i.e., not in the form of one who victimizes and enslaves the consciousness. The divine persona, in spite of and, even rather, through the surrender, frees the consciousness and fulfills it in its true identity.

The speaker wonders why his experience should be of demonic compulsion in the light of his conscious submission to God. But he does not seem to see that his "submission" is merely a manipulation of conscious images which he is thrusting upon his unconscious. "You should be showing your submissiveness to God (alias me, the speaker, the Lord-manipulator) and you aren't, you devil! Why not?" is another way to understand the implied message of the speaker's attitude. But the basic question is, rather, can the consciousness rightly manipulate one's unconscious (and hence one's whole psychic experience) in this arrogant way? The answer, of course, is that it cannot; or, at any rate, if it does, one's psyche is going to feel uncomfortable, and the man who tries is going to experience one part of himself (and, by implication, all of himself) in the form of a devil.

The fact that Donne (or I, in interpreting the poem) perceives the devil to be the persona of the unconscious is a superficial observation; the speaker and his "soul" are a convenient distinction for the sake of a language in which to express the experience of the discomfort. Because language is so important a part of our human nature, this convenience is also a necessity. But it should not be allowed to hide the fact that the speaker and the "soul," whether imitated here in a poem or as aspects of one's actual internal experience, are not nearly so distinct as Donne (or I) may at certain times make them out to be. The devil is just as truly the persona of the speaker as he is the persona of the unconscious. Is not the poem, perfectly clearly, an expression of self-blame? Is it not the speaker himself who is in league with the "world, the flesh, and the devil" but who, by not being able clearly to accept himself in this way, projects this demonic aspect of himself into his unconscious or, if the poem does not justify the term "unconscious," into some other "not-me" kind of reality? In this poem, Psyche, divided against herself, has not yet discovered her own real powers; that is why she bewails her lack of initiative; the marriage with God is not yet achieved. When it comes, she will no longer think of herself in this powerless way.

The apparent necessity for the initiative to come from God is indicated also in the second and twelfth sonnets. "Oh my blacke Soule! now thou art summoned," the speaker of the second sonnet begins, in terms of stern admonition. The soul is being brought up as if to the bar of justice on the last day, as if it is almost too late to begin a new life. There the speaker, who is also—but we shall not find it strange—the divine judge, directs the soul into the paths of righteousness with the voice of commanding authority, somewhat tempered by uncertainty and compassion. The soul is in desperate straits, like a treasonable escapee from justice who may receive the gift of life from the compassionate depths of the divine judge if only she will repent. But that presents a new problem, for the speaker wonders how the initiative for that repentance can come from such a sick soul:

> . . . grace, if thou repent, thou canst not lacke;
> But who shall give thee that grace to beginne?

The poem concludes with no intimation of a resolution to the speaker's question but rather only a further confirmation of his authority over his soul; he concludes by dictating the terms of the "gift" to the passive and hapless culprit his soul here appears to be:

> Oh make thy selfe with holy mourning blacke,
> And red with blushing, as thou art with sinne;
> Or wash thee in Christs blood, which hath this might
> That being red, it dyes red soules to white.

Although the soul is represented under the metaphor of a male person, it is certainly not shown as capable of any kind of aggressive role in relationship to the speaker, except in the same underground way that I have elucidated at more length in respect to the first sonnet.

In sonnet twelve the question comes to a clearer doctrinal focus, revolving around the problem of law and grace: whether a man can, by his own initiative, fulfill the conditions of the moral law. The speaker of the poem answers in the negative; only God's grace can do this:

> those laws, that men argue yet
> Whether a man those statutes can fulfill;
> None doth, but all-healing grace and Spirit,
> Revive againe what law and letter kill.
> Thy lawes abridgement, and thy last command
> Is all but love; Oh let that last Will stand!

The resolution is stated, but the poem scarcely imitates the experience which the doctrines describe. Only insofar as the tone of the final "Oh let that last Will stand!" represents the actual movement of love in the speaker rather than the attitude of imperious command does it recreate the experience.

Sonnet number eleven, "Wilt thou love God," points the way in which the true resolution will finally be achieved:

> Wilt thou love God, as he thee! Then digest,
> My Soule, this wholsome meditation,
> How God the Spirit, by Angels waited on
> In heaven, doth make his Temple in thy brest,
> The father having begot a Sonne most blest,
> And still begetting, (for he ne'r begonne)
> Hath deign'd to chuse thee by adoption,
> Coheire to'his glory,'and Sabbaths endlesse rest;
> And as a robb'd man, which by search doth finde
> His stolne stuffe sold, must lose or buy'it againe:
> The Sonne of glory came downe, and was slaine,
> Us whom he'had made, and Satan stolne, to unbinde.

This poem represents the mythic story of God's entry into the world. The entry begins with man's consciousness, which has been given its appropriate form through the bodily senses—hearing, reading, studying pictures. Sensory experience is the means by which the consciousness becomes identified with the body, i.e., it is how the consciousness is able to disclose itself in the form of the physical or external world. These images of the physical world are then sent from the consciousness into the unconscious for its meditation—in this poem, into the "soul." It is "wholsome" for the soul to ponder that God has made his dwelling place in "thy brest" and to understand that the begetting of the Christ child is a continuing occurrence. The speaker realizes that the historical event, coming to him in symbolic mediation through the external world, is also an image of what happens in his own actual psyche.

The incarnation is the central event of the story, as the final lines of the poem indicate:

> 'Twas much, that man was made like God before,
> But, that God should be made like man, much more.

How then does the eternal begetting of the divine-human son in the womb of man's flesh come about? The whole poem tells how, and the final lines rehearse the wonder of it—that the love which rises up in man's breast upon hearing the divine story and the love God has for man reflect each other. This reflection is the method of the eternal begetting. And one may accept that if he can accept "that God should be made like man." These words would suggest, for example, that, in accepting the power of love in oneself, one accepts God's love for oneself. But again, the acceptance must rise up from the unconscious, not merely be forced upon it by the consciousness.

Do we have an image of this unconscious acceptance in the last two lines of the poem? The answer would be "yes" if we understand the last two lines to represent the response of the soul to the speaker of the rest of the poem, and "no" if the speaker is the same throughout. My estimate is that the speaker of the rest of the lines joins with the soul in uttering these concluding lines, and they do, in a measure, therefore, express the love of God as a felt reality. The affectionate aspect of the lines, in that case, is the contribution, we may say, of the soul, and the doctrinal content is the contribution of the consciousness. The separation from himself which man suffers as a result of the fall from grace is healed by the incarnational event recreated in the language of this final couplet.

Although the last two lines of sonnet eleven do represent something like the psychic marriage as I have been describing it, the joining takes place without the marital

metaphor. A specifically sexual metaphor for the psychic
marriage appears among the Divine Meditations only in
"Batter my heart." Here we see the psyche as a woman
during the time of her alienation and discover that the end
of this separation will be a "marriage" between God and
the soul. That the "marriage" appears in the form of rape is
the result of the soul's incapacity, still, to see the signifi-
cance of the tremendous power implicit in its own de-
mands. "She" still pictures herself as helpless:

> Batter my heart, three person'd God; for, you
> As yet but knocke, breathe, shine, and seeke to mend;
> That I may rise, and stand, o'erthrow mee,'and bend
> Your force, to breake, blowe, burn and make me new.

Not only is this poem distinct among the Divine Medita-
tions in having a female persona for the soul, but—perhaps
connected with this—it is also distinct in that "she," the
soul—or, in Aristotelian terms, the affectionate faculty of
the soul—is the speaker, the "I" of the poem. This is shown
by the speaker's use of the third person in reference to
"Reason" in lines 7 and 8:

> I, like an usurpt towne, to'another due,
> Labour to'admit you, but Oh, to no end,
> Reason your viceroy in mee, mee should defend,
> But is captiv'd and proves weake or untrue.

And it is shown by the speaker's first person in respect to
"love" in line 9:

> Yet dearely'I love you, and would be lov'd faine,
> But am betroth'd unto your enemie.

The speaker understands herself betrayed by reason, who,
as God's viceroy, should have been standing guard for her

against the power of the devil "But is captiv'd, and proves weake or untrue." The town with its several "persons" (of whom, however, the poem mentions only two) is a metaphor for the one man, John Donne. The town is owed to God, but, through the weakness of reason, is in temporary control of the devil; nor can the speaker in the poem, who sees herself under reason's power, escape. To be sure, the speaker is not entirely stifled, since she may speak of the love of God as though she did love God; but neither is she satisfied, since she is still "betroth'd unto your enemie" and is therefore secured against a fruitful love affair with God.

In the octet the central image of the poem is impersonal: that town whose door needs to be battered down. But in the sestet the image is softened into something more personal and fleshly. The soul asks for God to take the intiative in the love affair, claiming to be too weak to remedy the situation, and the power God is to bring must be intense. The sestet as a whole reads:

> Yet dearely'I love you, and would be lov'd faine,
> But am betroth'd unto your enemie,
> Divorce mee,'untie, or breake that knot againe,
> Take mee to you, imprison mee, for I
> Except you'enthrall mee, never shall be free,
> Nor ever chast, except you ravish mee.

A love affair between God and man is present here and there throughout the Divine Meditations, although it is realized explicitly in male-female terms only in "Batter my heart," where the consummation is thwarted by the power of the devil. The important thing to see in these poems is that the marriage is at least being sought.

In the two long poems called the first and second *Anniversaries,* written in 1611 and 1612, Donne finally celebrates the marriage as an accomplished fact—an event simultaneous with the death and rebirth of the soul and simultaneous with his own rejoining the historical, or "material," world. He does so through the metaphor of the soul of Elizabeth Drury, whose death in December, 1610, was the occasion for these poems; she it was

> Who by a faithfull confidence, was here
> Betrothed to God, and now is married there.
>
> (*The Second Anniversarie*, ll. 461–62) [5]

and for whom Donne vows that he

> Will yearely celebrate thy second birth
> That is, thy death. For though the soule of man
> Be got when man is made, 'tis borne but than
> When man doth die. Our body's as the wombe,
> And as a mid-wife death directs it home.
>
> (*The First Anniversarie*, ll. 450–54)

The movement by which Elizabeth Drury's soul mirrors the soul of something other than herself is discoverable in the lines just quoted. But exactly who is Elizabeth Drury, or her soul, in these poems? Upon the answer to that question hinges the interpretation of the poems. Donne offers a clue in the subtitle to the *First Anniversarie*.

The *First Anniversarie* he subtitles *An Anatomy of the World. Wherein, by Occasion of the Untimely Death of Mistris Elizabeth Drury the Frailty and the Decay of this Whole World is Represented.* The poem describes the world as though it had lost its animating principle in the young girl's death, establishing the "she" of the poem as the *anima mundi.* But, by citing Donne's interpretation so

---

5. Frank Manley, ed., *John Donne: "The Anniversaries"* (Baltimore: Johns Hopkins Press, 1963), p. 106. All of my quotations from the *Anniversaries* are from Manley's edition. I have normalized the i's and j's and the u's and v's in quoting from Manley's text.

simply, I do not intend to deny several of the most pene-
trating other possibilities by which "she" may be explained;
for example, Donne also makes it clear that "she" is "vir-
tue." But the word "virtue" in its Latin roots means
"strength, power," and the *anima* of the world is its power.
This *anima mundi* is also connected to the *logos,* as Emp-
son says, and "wisdom," as Manley interprets; for wisdom
and *logos* are each traditionally identified with the second
person of the Trinity, the creative power of the world.[6]
Nevertheless, some of these identifications, since they are
more Scholastic than mythic, are a little misleading. Man-
ley points in the right direction when he says, in his
introduction to his edition of the *Anniversaries,* that

> symbols . . . resist all efforts at precise, intellectual defini-
> tion. But in present-day terms perhaps a vague idea of what
> Donne was getting at is available in C. G. Jung's concept
> of the *anima,* which is in itself vague, but which in general
> represents the "Idea of a Woman" in man, the image of his
> own soul, his own deepest reality. It is a universal symbol
> of otherness in man, either of desire, the completion of
> one's own androgynous self, as in the Platonic myth, or of
> strange intuitive knowledge otherwise unavailable to him,
> "a source of information about things for which a man has
> no eyes." [7]

The "Idea of a Woman" is Donne's own explanation, and,
as Manley notes, this is reminiscent of Platonic as well as
Jungian language. It will not come as a surprise to students

6. For the *Logos,* the "Word," in the King James version see
John 1:1 ff. For wisdom see Proverbs 8, esp. verses 22 ff. For the
creative power of the world see Colossians 1:15 ff.
7. Frank Manley, *John Donne: "The Anniversaries,"* p. 18. I
am indebted to Mr. Manley for much of the information in this
paragraph. The passage Manley quotes at the conclusion of the
excerpt cited he footnotes to *Two Essays in Analytical Psychology,*
trans. R. F. C. Hull, Vol. VII of *The Collected Works of C. G.
Jung,* ed. H. Read, M. Fordham, and G. Adler, Bollingen Series
XX (New York: Pantheon Books, 1953), p. 186.

of Plato that the *Symposium,* where the myth of androgynous man is found, contains also an account of a psychic marriage which compares "souls which are pregnant" to "those who are pregnant in the body only" and speaks of "children" of the kind which Homer and Hesiod have begotten.[8] Of course, the rebirth of the spirit is also biblical, best known perhaps from Nicodemus' objection to Jesus: "How can a man be born when he is old? Can he enter the second time into his mother's womb and be born?" To which Jesus answers, "That which is born of the flesh is flesh, and that which is born of the Spirit is spirit. Do not marvel that I said to you, 'you must be born anew.' " [9] It is implicit also in the resurrection archetype and is found here and there in the Epistles.[10] The answer to the question of exactly what Elizabeth Drury, or her soul, refers to in these poems can only be that "she" does not refer *exactly* to anything. She refers to several "things" in varying degrees of metaphoric extension. I must put the word "thing" in quotation marks so that we will not make the error of imagining that because several words are used to express who "she" is, or several kinds of historic context supplied to elucidate her meanings, these metaphoric relationships could not reflect real mutual participation. The psyche is not exactly a "thing." But identifying "her" as the *anima mundi* and relating her to Jungian and Platonic archetypes of the psyche has this much to recommend it over some of the others: it does not require switching into masculine a gender clearly feminine throughout the poem.

Since the psyche of individual man participates in the general psyche of the world, if the *anima mundi* is lost, man is dead; and no live readers of poems celebrating this death can be found to profit by it. Donne is aware of this

8. *Symposium* 208–9.
9. John 3:1 ff. (RSV).
10. See, e.g., Col. 2:12 f.; I Pet. 1:3; I John 4:7, 5:18.

problem. He resolves it in the *First Anniversarie* by denying the absoluteness of the death of the world, just as in his own personal life the "death" he spoke of was a metaphorical death, in which some kind of life remained behind to preserve his body from putrefaction.

> Let no man say, the world it selfe being dead,
> 'Tis labour lost to have discovered
> The worlds infirmities, since there is none
> Alive to study this dissectione;
> For there's a kind of world remaining still,
> Though shee which did inanimate and fill
> The world, be gone, yet in this last long night,
> Her Ghost doth walke; that is, a glimmering light,
> A faint weake love of vertue and of good
> Reflects from her, on them which understood
> Her worth; And though she have shut in all day,
> The twi-light of her memory doth stay;
> Which, from the carcasse of the old world, free,
> Creates a new world; and new creatures be
> Produc'd: The matter and the stuffe of this,
> Her vertue, and the forme our practise is.
>
> (ll. 63–78)

"This body of death" (to use Saint Paul's phrase for our somatic character) [11] is never so absolutely dead that it does not also contain the germinative cells from which new life may ever spring. "To the mortal creature, generation is a sort of eternity and immortality," says Plato,[12] and so does John Donne in nearly that same language in the *Essays in Divinity*.[13]

For Donne, "her" action in separating herself from the

---

11. Romans 7:24 (RSV).
12. *Symposium* 206.
13. Donne, *Essays in Divinity*, ed. Simpson, p. 69. Donne there says, "Propagation is the truest Image and nearest representation of eternity."

earth and then shedding back some luster from her virtue is imitable, and it is this imitation by those who remember her which keeps alive the world; it is the means by which the immortal seed is planted so as to bring about the new birth of the world. Thus, in the *Second Anniversarie,* subtitled *Of the Progres of the Soule. Wherein: By Occasion of the Religious Death of Mistris Elizabeth Drury, the Incommodities of the Soule in This Life and her Exaltation in the Next, are Contemplated,* Donne shows us such an imitation of the action of Elizabeth Drury's death; his soul mounts up into heaven in meditation, and he describes that meditation in his poem. He first meditates on how unfortunate his soul is while tied down to his body on earth:

> Thinke in how poore a prison thou didst lie
> After [birth], enabled but to sucke, and crie.

> (ll. 173–74)

He then contrasts this with the freeing of the soul in death:

> But thinke that Death hath now enfranchis'd thee,
> Thou hast thy'expansion now and libertee;
> . . . .
> And thinke this slow-pac'd soule, which late did cleave,
> To'a body, and went but by the bodies leave,
> Twenty, perchance, or thirty mile a day,
> Dispatches in a minute all the way,
> Twixt Heaven, and Earth.

> (ll. 179–89)

He imagines his soul going up past the moon and all the intermediate spheres between here and there,

> So by the soule doth death string Heaven and Earth,
> For when our soule enjoyes this her third birth,
> (Creation gave her one, a second, grace,)
> Heaven is as neare, and present to her face,

As colours are, and objects, in a roome
Where darknesse was before, when Tapers come.

(ll. 213–18)

Between the *First* and the *Second Anniversarie* Donne de-
cided to count physical death as a third rather than a second
birth. That he now refers to the imaginative death as the
soul's second birth among three raises the suggestion that
the middle always raises in relation to any pair of manner-
ist polarities. If the first birth be of the soul into the body
and the third be of the soul into heaven, then the second
birth, grace, is what reconciles the two. Or if the first birth
be understood to derive chiefly from this world, the secular
order, and the third from the other world, the eternal order,
then the middle—obtained in meditation—derives chiefly
from a structure which joins this world to the other, the
temporal to the eternal, and is represented here by the
poem.

The *Anniversaries* celebrate the divine marriage by rec-
onciling the most profound polarities in man's experience,
symbolized chiefly in the polarities of death and birth but
including also this world and the other world, heaven and
earth, God and man, the eternal and the temporal. Does
the marriage take place through God's initiative or
Donne's? The images of the *Anniversaries,* and of the Di-
vine Meditations, tend more in the direction of God's initia-
tive, but engaging in meditation and writing poetry are
taken at the initiative of the poet. Probably the best answer,
at least at the level at which I have been treating these
subjects, is to regard the "metaphorical marriage" as just
that, a "marriage" whose meaning is best explained
through its metaphor, that is, as it is in its natural exem-
plar. What that is in its fuller meanings I leave to the
reader; but I might start him off by suggesting that a
marriage is a cooperative action in which each partner must

relate to the other as if the other were dominant—to which I add, however, by way of giving mystery, depth, and reality to my own words, that neither one is to allow his right hand to know what his left hand is doing.

Elizabeth Drury's marriage to God and Donne's are the same because "she" and the *anima mundi* are identified. That Donne's soul has been able to activate his body to imitate her in a meditative poem *is* virtue, not merely a reflection of it. "She" is the

> blessed maid,
> Of whom is meant what ever hath beene said,
> Or shall be spoken well by any tongue,
> Whose name refines course lines, and makes prose song.
>
> *(The First Anniversarie,* ll. 443–46)

When Ben Jonson objected that "if it had been written of ye Virgin Marie it had been something," [14] Donne might have replied that unless the Virgin Mary were imitable later in time, as by Elizabeth Drury, God would now have no way to join history. The poems, imitating Elizabeth Drury in turn, also represent God's way of joining the world.

Like Ben Jonson, Donne himself found fault with the *Anniversaries,* but it was in neither the writing nor the subject matter; it was that he had printed them. All the meanings of the psychic marriage were not yet fulfilled in him, and the joining of private to public spiritual expression still seemed distasteful. Yet the very awkwardness of the joining of the private to the public, of the inner to the outer, is the mark of the mannerist style. So also is the strained metaphor of Elizabeth Drury's soul as the *anima mundi.* Certainly these metaphors are inappropriate. But,

14. Quoted from Manley, *John Donne: "The Anniversaries,"* p. 7.

had Donne chosen the Virgin Mary as a more appropriate, public, and publishable metaphor, could he have joined his own *anima,* the only part of the *anima mundi* over which he could have direct experience and control, to its own place and time in history as well as he did by choosing the little-known Elizabeth Drury? For the celebration of her marriage to God made it possible for Donne to link the depths of his own inner life to the Drury family. It is this link which establishes the importance of the poem for Donne's biography and by which the reality of the psychic story is confirmed. Elizabeth Drury was the daughter of Sir Robert Drury, and by writing the *Anniversarie* of her death Donne hoped to secure Sir Robert as his patron—and did. Through the poem celebrating her marriage to God, "she" was indeed born anew—in the person of the author, who was adopted into the very household which Sir Robert's daughter had vacated.

Gosse did not understand Donne's connection with the Drurys. He found it so much "the most mysterious element in his condition at this time" that he was "tempted to think the lodgings in Drury House a myth." [15] He said they were so tenuously founded "on the whim of Sir Robert Drury" [16] that he supposed "Donne had already given up his rooms in Drury House" [17] before Sir Robert died on April 2, 1615, little more than two months after Donne was ordained. Since the publication of R. C. Bald's *Donne and the Drurys* in 1959,[18] however, we know a great deal more about this connection than Gosse did. To attest its actuality, Bald has added a host of detail, mostly from business records of the Drury family, and it adds up to a substantial

---

15. Gosse, *Life,* II, 53.
16. *Ibid.,* p. 4.
17. *Ibid.,* p. 92.
18. R. C. Bald, *Donne and the Drurys* (Cambridge, Eng.: At the University Press, 1959).

picture. We know that Walton's earlier account of a separate residence for Donne on the Drury property is the correct one, not his revision showing both families sharing the Drury mansion. We know with great probability just where Donne's house was located on the grounds and its size in respect to Sir Robert's residence; and although Bald is not sure that Donne had the house rent-free, it is impossible to believe that he did not receive some kind of financial aid from his patron.

The length and intimacy of Donne's connection with the family is also shown in the records Bald has gathered. The settlement of his estate made by Sir Robert on May 19, 1613, and still effective at the time of his death, names John Donne as a trustee equally in this respect with a Mr. Clement Paman and with Sir Henry Drury, Sir Robert's second cousin.[19] After the death of her husband, Lady Drury remained on good enough terms with Donne that he was, on March 20, 1617, a witness to "two indentures which Brooke signed with Lady Drury," his name being listed between two others of the Drury family.[20] Because Christopher Brooke had been a friend since the days when he attended Donne's wedding and was now his daily associate at Lincoln's Inn, Bald believes it likely that Donne brought Brooke and Lady Drury together.[21] And finally, we know that Donne lived in his "house at Drury House" until he left it to occupy the deanery of Saint Paul's in 1621.[22] So far from its being tenuously founded on Sir Robert's whim alone, not to speak of Gosse's suspicion that it might all have been a myth, Donne's relationship with the Drurys survived Sir Robert's death by six years if we date the conclusion by his leaving the Drury property; and thus

19. *Ibid.,* pp. 142–43.
20. *Ibid.,* p. 154.
21. *Ibid.*
22. *Ibid.,* p. 119. The quote is from Donne (*ibid.,* p. 120).

what began in 1611, through Donne's writing a poem on the death of fifteen-year-old Elizabeth Drury, lasted at least ten years. But even from the beginning this connection improved Donne's prospects. In the latter part of 1611, possibly before the first of the poems was published, he had already set forth on a quasi-diplomatic mission with Sir Robert which placed him on the fringes of the most important affairs of state. And now for the first time since his marriage of the flesh in 1601 he had gained a foothold from which a practical effort to scale the heights of church and state could be attempted.

Donne was at last giving up his uncommitted stance. The invisible church is not enough for man living in the visible world. The time had come for Donne to make his attempt at climbing the hill of truth. In this effort it was indeed "no small part, that shee,"

> who by making full perfection grow,
> Peeces a Circle, and still keepes it so,
> Long'd for, and longing for'it, to heaven is gone,
> Where shee receives, and gives addition.
>
> (*The Second Anniversarie*, ll. 507–10)

It was just the "addition" he needed. By means of her marriage to God, John Donne was reborn in the world.

CHAPTER VII

CHURCH
AND STATE

In 1612, shortly after his trip to the Continent with Sir Robert Drury, Donne wrote a letter to the young man then in the position most likely to secure favors from King James, Rochester, the Earl of Somerset:

> Having obeyed at last, after much debatement within me, the inspirations (as I hope) of the Spirit of God, and re- solved to make my profession Divinity; I made account, that I do but tell your Lordship, what God hath told me, which is, that it is in this course, if in any, that my service may be of use to this Church and State. Since then your Lordship's virtues have made you so near the head in the one, and so religious a member of the other, I came to this courage, of thrusting myself thus into your Lordship's presence.[1]

This is the first time in all of our story that Donne had expressed any intention to find his vocation in the church.

1. Gosse, *Life,* II, 20–21.

This apparently sudden decision and the channels through which he went to realize it have raised several questions. Did Donne have any genuine vocation to the ministry? Was he really a convinced Anglican? Did his character suffer "deterioration," as Gosse said, by his associations with the Rochester scandal or by his continuing to seek preferment from the court? We can answer these questions only by trying to reconstruct the movement of his attitudes as they led up to his ordination.

That Donne wrote this letter to Rochester merely to seek financial gain is not a serious charge, although his own words can be construed to give it some support. In the letter to Lord Hay which enclosed the letter to Rochester quoted above, Donne wrote,

> I have brought all my distractions together, and find them in a resolution of making divinity my profession, that I may try whether my poor studies, which have profited me nothing, may profit others in that course; in which also a fortune may either be better made, or, at least, better missed, than in any other.[2]

Our interpretation of this passage depends on how we understand the word "fortune." It cannot simply mean money. Not only had Donne refused Morton's earlier proposals, but the years of his worst poverty had been 1607–11, and by the time of his appeal to Rochester the tide had turned; he had entered into the service of Sir Robert Drury. Furthermore, as early as 1609 he had begun to receive the dowry so long withheld by his obstinate and angry father-in-law. The word primarily alludes to his fortune in the world, that is, the court; for, as the letter to Rochester shows, Donne was fully aware that his effort to secure a religious vocation from this source was an effort to join himself more expressly to church and state.

2. *Ibid.,* p. 22.

During the Continental trip Donne had considered tak-
ing up law upon his return, as an account of a letter written
by Donne to Morton at this time shows:

> The said Mr. Donne, having grappled with many extremi-
> ties at home, he passed over into France, where he gave
> himself to study of the laws. And from Amiens (as I
> remember) he wrote a letter to his always true friend Dean
> Morton, wherein he requested his advice whether the tak-
> ing of the degree of a doctor in that profession of the laws,
> it might be conducible and advantageous unto him to
> practise at home in the Arches, London.[3]

Gosse saw this letter to Morton as a sign of how uninter-
ested Donne was in the church right up until a swift and
complete reversal came about. "Nowhere is he so little of a
divine as in these years immediately preceding his sudden
resolution to enter the Church," says Gosse;[4] but he omitted
the last sentence of the account, which shows Dean Mor-
ton's response:

> Unto whom the *Deane* then returned him answer, That in
> his Judgement, he thought the Ministry in the Church of
> God would be safer, and fitter for him: Whereupon he
> desisted from further prosecution of those Studies.[5]

One might ask why a man indifferent to a church vocation
should write for advice from a friend who had once
strongly urged him to take orders, a friend himself now
become dean of Winchester. Would he not have suspected

3. The text is taken from an account of Morton's life written
by his secretary, Richard Baddeley. I have quoted it from Gosse,
Life, I, 304, where the full source is given.
4. *Ibid.,* p. 305.
5. Evelyn M. Simpson, *A Study of the Prose Works of John
Donne,* 2d ed. (Oxford: Oxford University Press, 1948), p. 25.
I have quoted this sentence from Baddeley's complete account,
given by Simpson, who also footnotes Gosse's failure to take note
of the context.

what Morton's reply would be? But if I seem to be suggesting that law was a purely "secular" vocation contrasted to a purely "sacred" calling, I am misrepresenting the situation. The law at this time was of course still deeply intertwined with divinity, nor did the sacredness of divinity set it over against the secular order. After his ordination Donne was himself for more than two years the reader in divinity to the benchers of Lincoln's Inn. The benchers, or lawyers, were the same men who, according to Gosse, had known him from his very boyhood [6] and among whom he might well have been sitting and hearing sermons from another preacher had he chosen the law. The difference was a matter of focus and of role, not of an entirely different life orientation. Donne's aim at this time was to find his way into the service of his king. Certainly. Yet, even if Donne had still considered himself a Roman Catholic, such an aim would not have signified a choice between secular and sacred employment. But because he had been an Anglican privately at least since 1609, and publicly at least since the publication of *Pseudo-Martyr* in 1610, such an aim did not even signify a choice between church and state.

Many commentators point out that Donne during this period sought a post as ambassador, as if this also represented a stiff-backed choice exclusive of the church. But in fact, four years *after* he was ordained, he finally achieved something close to this goal: he accompanied Doncaster, who was his old friend, Lord Hay, on an embassy to Germany. According to Gosse, Donne was appointed to this embassy directly by King James, and his mission was not merely that of chaplain. Though Gosse thought that the post was given to Donne to improve his health, he says that Donne was directed to " 'assist' Doncaster with his 'conversation and discourse,' " and that "nothing was said,

6. Gosse, *Life,* II, 111.

and certainly nothing appears to have been done, in the direction of secretarial work." [7] Furthermore, to cite an example in reverse, when Sir Henry Wotton, another of Donne's friends, returned to England after many years abroad as ambassador, he sought for and received ordination and service in the Church of England as one aspect of his settling down into the service of his own country at home.[8]

The trip abroad with Drury, prior to his ordination, led Donne into closer court associations than he had had for ten years. During the time of this trip, France was without her ambassador from England, Sir Henry Wotton, with whom, however, Donne was in close contact. Sir Robert Drury's trip, though without official authorization, was looked upon favorably by those in court circles. No doubt the intention of the trip was to gain this favor for Sir Robert, who probably hoped for Sir Henry's position; and that it was at least partly successful in this way is shown by the attitude expressed by Sir Walter Cope, the lord treasurer's physician, who wrote Drury on May 12, 1612:

> Although Mr Dun, and you have noe place of Ambassadors yet I trust you have, that canne and doe observe as much as the best that have imploiement from the State, and it will be noe ill Introduction towards the setting such idle persons on worke; . . . . I commend [to you] my service; not forgetting my best commendation to Mr. Donne, who is inriching his Treasury, for his Countries better service, towards the which, if I be not able to add a mite, yet I shall be ever ready to cry Amen.[9]

7. *Ibid.,* p. 120.
8. Augustus Jessop makes this observation in connection with Donne's decision in *John Donne: Sometime Dean of St. Paul's, A.D. 1621–1631* (Boston: Houghton Mifflin, 1897), p. 87.
9. R. C. Bald, *Donne and the Drurys* (Cambridge, Eng.: At the University Press, 1959), p. 100. I have normalized the u's and v's, i's and j's, in quoting this passage.

Cope's English is awkward. His sense is: "You and John Donne do not have the formal title of ambassador, but you do have the kind of position from which you can perform (and are performing) the duties of the office, and indeed your activities are a good example to many idle persons who hold the official titles." Donne's court prospects also were distinctly encouraged by this trip abroad, as that letter shows. But since an interest in court connections did not signify lack of interest in ecclesiastical ones, we should not be surprised to find that Donne came the closest on that trip to playing a role in French-English diplomatic relations when he attempted to strengthen the Gallican wing of French Catholicism.

But does this effort show that Donne's Anglicanism was insecure at this time, that he still hankered after Roman Catholicism? Certainly not, if by Roman Catholicism we mean acknowledging the pope as head of the church, as the letter describing the incident shows. He is writing Sir Henry Goodyer:

> You must of necessity have heard often of a book written against the Pope's jurisdiction, about three months since, by one Richer, a doctor and syndic of the Sorbonists, which book hath now been censured by an assembly of the clergy of this archbishopric. . . .
>
> Richer was first accused to the Parliament, but when it was there required of his delators to insist upon some propositions in his book, which were either against Scripture or the Gallican Church, they desisted in that pursuit. . . . Almost all the curates of the parishes of Paris being Sorbonists, there is by this means a strong party of the Sorbonists themselves raised against Richer; yet against this censure, and against three or four which have opposed Richer in print, he meditates an answer.
>
> Before it should come forth I desired to speak with him, for I had said to some of the Sorbonists of his party that there was no proposition in his book which I could not show in Catholic authors of 300 years: I had from him an

assignation to meet, and at the hour he sent me his excuse, which was that he had been traduced to have had conference with the ambassadors of England and the States, and with the Duke of Bouillon, and that he had accepted a pension of the King of England; and withal, that it had been very well testified to him that day that the Jesuits had offered to corrupt men with rewards to kill him. Which I doubt not but he apprehended for true, because a messenger whom I sent to fix another time of meeting with him, found him in an extreme trembling and irresolutions; so that I had no more but an entreaty to forbear coming to his house, or drawing him out of it, till it might be without danger or observation.[10]

From this letter it seems that there was a split between a Gallican and a papal group of Catholic churchmen. The Gallican group, among whom Richer was one, wanted to limit the pope's jurisdiction. Any such limitation, of course, would have the effect of strengthening the French king, and the splinter group of Sorbonists had to be careful not to seem to infringe on the royal power when they censured Richer. But in fact Richer and the majority of the Sorbonists were on the side of the king's authority in the dispute, and the others on the side of the pope's. In this quarrel Donne steps in to support Richer, saying to the others that Richer's is the true Catholic position, as can be supported by references to their own recent literature as well as by the Bible and the councils of the Early Fathers.

The Gallican wing of the French church, though it remained in communion with Rome, was nearly identical in its antipapism with the Anglican. Donne's *Pseudo-Martyr,* like Richer's book, was also written against the pope's jurisdiction. There is no reason for wonderment why the Anglican Donne would have sympathized with the Gallican Catholic Richer; the wonder should arise had he not sympathized with such a nationalized form of Christianity.

10. Gosse, *Life,* I, 296–97.

Naturally a man who had chosen to support English against Roman Catholicism would support French against Roman. At issue is the role of the king.

But how much of his own moral integrity will a man sacrifice to support his king? This is the question that emerges over Donne's relationship to the court favorite, to whom he had written that letter in 1612, hoping through him to gain the king's ear. The story is long and complex, and it has never been told correctly.

In describing Donne's supposed complicity in the obnoxious Rochester affair, Gosse found three things to identify: "nullity, re-marriage, epithalamium." [11] The first refers to the nullity suit which freed Lady Howard from her husband; the second refers to her marriage to Rochester on December 26, 1613. These events took place several years before the lovers were found guilty in the more serious affair of murder. The grounds of the nullity were sufficiently dubious that approval was given for it only reluctantly, and it was least supported by persons of the most repute, such as Lancelot Andrewes. Gosse thought that Donne had been secured, and that he acted, as legal counsel for the nullity suit, but he mistook for John Donne a Sir Daniell Dunn.[12] That much of Gosse's charges against Donne has been disposed of for some years. What yet remains is Donne's support of the marriage, particularly as indicated by his having written an epithalamium for it. Gosse found the poem "extremely disconcerting" and said that "it is very difficult to approach this poem without a strong feeling of repulsion." The best he can find to say is that, since poets are afflicted by a "strange blindness" in such matters, we can find something to Donne's credit in

11. *Ibid.,* II, 24.
12. Simpson, *A Study of the Prose Works of John Donne,* pp. 29–30.

the fact that "on the same winter morning Ben Jonson handed to 'virtuous Somerset' a copy of verses even more enthusiastic than those of Donne." As for the poem itself, he says that, "if . . . we forget the occasion for which it was composed, it may be read with considerable pleasure."[13] Grierson follows Gosse's insinuations in this aspect of his relationship to Rochester, adding, after he has freed Donne of complicity in the nullity suit, "none the less, Donne's own letters show that he was quite willing to lend a hand in promoting the divorce; and that before the decree was granted he was already busy polishing his epithalamium."[14]

But Donne's poem is surely one of the most reluctant, ambiguous epithalamiums ever written. Nor does it detract from the poem or from Donne's character to consider the circumstances under which it was composed, particularly its supposed early date, on which hangs the most persuasive accusation of his fawning at court. These circumstances are, as Grierson indicates, largely deduced from Donne's letters, and most importantly from two of them which talk about his own and others' poems on that marriage. One of these letters is written to Sir Robert Ker, a friend of Donne's at the court, whose Christian and family name is by chance the same as Rochester's. Donne begins his letter as follows: "Sir,—I had rather like the first best; not only because it is cleanlier, but because it reflects least upon the other party, which, in all jest and earnest, in this affair, I wish avoided."[15] Since the next sentence of the letter refers to the possibility that he himself would write an epithalamium, it seems likely that this first sentence alludes to the

13. Gosse, *Life*, II, 31–33.
14. Herbert J. C. Grierson, *The Poems of John Donne*, 2 vols. (Oxford: Oxford University Press, 1912), II, 94.
15. Gosse, *Life*, II, 26–27.

first of a group of several poems which Sir Robert had sent to him to comment upon. Donne's criticism of these indicates his attitude: he likes "the first best, . . . because it reflects least upon the other party." I suppose the other party is the Lady Howard's former husband, the Earl of Essex, and Donne is sensitive enough to the problems in the nullity action to wish to avoid such reflections. In the next two sentences he says, "If my muse were only out of fashion, and but wounded and maimed like free-will in the Roman Church, I should adventure to put her to an epithalamium. But since she is dead, like free-will in our Church, I have not so much muse left as to lament her loss." [16] To be sure, this letter cannot be exactly dated, but these sentences show that, at the time others are doing so, Donne specifically rejects the intention to write an epithalamium.

The other letter is dated "Jan. 19" and is printed by Gosse as though addressed to a person with the initials "G. K." Gosse believed himself forced to date this letter January 19, 1613, almost a full year before the actual marriage on December 26 of that year, because, he said, "by that day of 1614 everything was long over, nullity, remarriage, epithalamium, and all." [17] Gosse makes no effort to identify this "G. K.," which he has reprinted from the *Letters* of 1651, and Charles Edmund Merrill, Jr., the modern editor of the letters, says, "I am unable to identify *G. K.*" [18] No other letter addressed to anyone of the initials "G. K." is printed by Gosse (nor are there any in the *Letters* of 1651). I venture to claim that the letter was almost

16. *Ibid.,* p. 27.
17. *Ibid.,* p. 24.
18. *Letters to Severall Persons of Honour by John Donne,* edited, with notes, by Charles Edmund Merrill, Jr. (New York: Sturgis & Walton, 1910), p. 299.

certainly written in 1614 and should be addressed to "G. B."
rather than "G. K." Let us examine the evidence for this
assertion. I begin by quoting the letter in full, exactly as
printed by Gosse, including the postscript, which is the clue
Gosse missed to the correct dating and addressee:

To my worthy friend G. K.

SIR,—I receive this here that I begin this return, your
letter by a servant of Sir G. Greseley, by whom also I hasten
this despatch. This needs no enlargement, since it hath the
honour to convey one from Mr. Gerrard. But though by
telling me it was a bold letter, I had leave to open it, and
that I have a little itch to make some animadversions and
criticisms upon it (as that there is a cypher too much in
the sum of the King's debts, and such like), yet since my
eyes do easily fall back to their distemper, and that I am
this night to sup at Sir Ar. Ingram's, I had rather forfeit
their little strength at his supper than with writing such
impertinencies; the best spending them is upon the rest of
your letter, to which, Sir, I can only say in general that
some appearances have been here of some treatise concern-
ing this nullity, which are said to proceed from Geneva, but
are believed to have been done within doors, by encourage-
ments of some whose names I will not commit to this
letter.

My poor study having lain that way, it may prove
possible that my weak assistance may be of use in this
matter in a more serious fashion than an epithalamium.
This made me therefore abstinent in that kind; yet, by my
troth, I think I shall not escape. I deprehend in myself more
than an alacrity, a vehemency to do service to that com-
pany, and so I may find reason to make rhyme. If it be
done, I see not how I can admit that circuit of sending
them to you to be sent hither; that seems a kind of praying
to saints, to whom God must tell first that such a man prays
to them to pray to Him. So that I shall lose the honour of
that conveyance, but for recompense you shall escape the
danger of approving it. My next letter shall say more of

this. This shall end with delivering you the remembrance
of my Lady Bartlett, who is present at the sealing hereof.

Your very true and affectionate servant,

J. Donne.

Jan. 19 [1613].

Which name, when there is any empty corner in your
discourse with that noble lady at Ashby, I humbly beseech
you to present to her as one more devoted to her service
than perchance you will say.[19]

Notice Donne's ambiguity of tone. He protests in this
letter that he has "more than an alacrity, a vehemency to
do service to that company, and so I may find reason to
make rhyme," and yet at the same time assures that, should
the poem be written, his correspondent "shall escape the
danger of approving it." What kind of poem can it be that
will both do service to "that company" (Rochester, the
Lady Howard, and those furthering their affairs) and yet
will be in danger of being disapproved? Furthermore, what
is Donne's relationship with a correspondent to whom he
expresses loyalty to Rochester but whom he does not wish
to make the bearer of his poem and upon whose letter he
has a "little itch to make some animadversions and criti-
cisms"? But let us continue.

This letter contained another, enclosed within it, for Mr.
Gerrard. On pages 30–36 of the second volume of Gosse's
Life and Letters is printed a set of three letters, all to a "Sir
G. B." The dates and subject matter of all three are inter-
locked; they were written at the close of 1613 and the
opening of the next year. Two of them show great concern

19. Gosse, *Life*, II, 24–25. Gosse has apparently emended the
original "heare," of the first line of this letter, to "here." Merrill
prints "heare" and conjectures its meaning to be "hour," which
seems to me better than Gosse's emendation (*Letters to Severall
Persons*, p. 155).

with a matter of personal hostility between Donne and G. B. which had arisen as a result of G. B.'s interpretation of a letter from Mr. Gerard *and of a certain postscript contained in a letter from Donne.* That postscript is obviously the one in the letter quoted in full above, and that other letter clearly belongs to this set of three letters. Here is the passage from the letter to Sir G. B. which alludes to the postscript:

> SIR, even in the letter itself to me I deprehend much inclination to chide me, and it is but out of your habit of good language that you spare me. So little occasion as that postscript of mine could not bring you so near to it, if nothing else were mistaken, which (so God help me) was so little that I remember not what it was, and I would no more hear again what I write in an officious letter than what I said at a drunken supper. I had no purpose to exercise your diligence in presenting my name to that lady, but either I did, or should have said that I writ only to fill up any empty corner in your discourse.

Consider also the next two sentences, referring to the way Sir G. B. had interpreted Donne to Mr. Gerrard as a result of Mr. Gerrard's letter. In no letter of Donne's does his own tone show such asperity (there is no break between this and the previous quote):

> So, Sir, the reading of the letter was a kind of travail to me, but when I came to the paper enclosed I was brought to bed of a monster.
> To express myself vehemently quickly, I must say that I can scarce think that you have read Mr. Gerrard's letter rightly, therefore I send you back your own again.

The letter continues with more angry defense against G. B.'s personal indictments, concluding:

> Sixteen letters from Mr. Gerrard could not (I think)
> persuade a Middlesex jury of so much dishonesty in
> > Your true servant,
> > J. Donne.[20]

This letter is undated, but the one preceding it in the series
is dated December 23, conjectured by Gosse to be in 1613,
and the one succeeding it, and clearly belonging to the
personal controversy, is firmly dated *"Sat. 12 Feb.
1613[4]."* Donne dated the year according to the old style;
hence this "1613" means "1614" according to the present
dating, as Gosse rightly indicates. When one fixes the letter
of January 19 into the series, it is surely the one whose
postscript and enclosed letter from Mr. Gerrard started the
kettle seething, and its date should be January 19, 1614.
The whole series reveals a sequence of dates as follows. I
give the dates exactly as Gosse did, save for the crucial
letter of January 19, of course, which Gosse wrongly dated
1613 and which I have therefore revised to 1614:

> Dec. 23 [1613]
> Jan. 19 [1614]
> [Feb. 1614?]
> Sat. 12 Feb. 1613 [1614]

Why did Gosse ascribe to this letter a date which was
a whole year too early? Perhaps he was misled by the
"G. K." printed in the *Letters* of 1651; but that could have
little to do with its date. The reference to "this nullity"
would seem to have been made at the time the suit was
pending, but only if one had already made up one's mind
about the date. The only likely explanation is that Gosse
was attempting to support his view that John Donne's
interest in becoming ordained represented a sudden conver-
sion. Thus he ends the chapter called "Last Years as a
Layman":

20. Gosse, *Life*, II, 35–36.

The whole of this period in Donne's life was ignominious, and his dependence upon Somerset degrading to his judgment and conscience. The reader cannot fail to observe a temporary deterioration of his character. Poverty and anxiety dragged this beautiful nature down into the dust. But a complete relief was now coming, and a startling change in the whole order and tenor of his being. His life as a layman was about to be abruptly closed.[21]

But Donne's reference to "this nullity" does not require us to believe it was not a *fait accompli* at the time of his letter. The treatise referred to can certainly just as well have been written about the already completed suit, possibly some ex post facto justification of the decree or the report which had been written by Sir Daniell Dunn during or prior to the proceedings. Now that we know that this important letter is to be dated in 1614, what we see is that, almost a full month after the marriage, Donne has still not written his epithalamium but feels that he might yet have to.

The poem itself contains evidence of its tardy composition and shows other important matters bearing on Donne's attitude toward the marriage. The date of the wedding, which could hardly have been known almost a year earlier, before the nullity suit had even been granted, is woven right into the texture of the poem. The "Ecclogue" into which the epithalamium proper is set starts by identifying the date of the marriage, December 26, 1613, and the opening stanza of the epithalamium, labeled indeed *"The time of the Mariage,"* begins:

> Thou art repriv'd old yeare, thou shalt not die,
>   Though thou upon thy death bed lye,
>   And should'st within five days expire.[22]

21. *Ibid.,* p. 54.
22. The quotations from Donne's epithalamium are from Grierson, *The Poems of John Donne,* I, 131–41.

Could Donne have composed all but these few lines a year earlier, inserting them only when the date of the wedding was announced? But the argument of the whole of the "Ecclogue" is a defense of the poet's absence from court on the day of the wedding:

> Allophanes *finding* Idios *in the country in Christmas time, reprehends his absence from court, at the mariage Of the Earle of Somerset,* Idios *gives an account of his purpose therein, and of his absence thence.*

Idios, Greek for "the private man, who has no place at court," is clearly Donne, and Allophanes, "one who seems like another," is probably Sir Robert Ker, a nobleman at court and a friend of Donne's whose name was identical with the bridegroom's.[23] Allophanes concludes the "Ecclogue" by reminding Idios that, since the king has taken this man (the bridegroom) to his heart, he who fails to join with Cupid at the marriage loses access to "that brest Where the Kings Counsells and his secrets rest." Idios replies that he did not want to appear at the wedding feast without his "Grace," that is, his poem, ready:

> I knew
> All this, and onely therefore I withdrew.
> To know and feele all this, and not to have
>   Words to expresse it, makes a man a grave
> Of his owne thoughts; I would not therefore stay
>   At a great feast, having no Grace to say.

However, he argues, now that he has failed the occasion and has lost access to the king thereby, he can say something which cannot be accused of flattery. His loss is "death," his words the epitaph, and the poem celebrates Rochester's marriage through that sacrificial offering:

23. *Ibid.,* II, 94.

And yet I scap'd not here; for being come
Full of the common joy, I utter'd some;
Reade then this nuptiall song, which was not made
Either the Court or mens hearts to invade,
But since I'am dead, and buried, I could frame
No Epitaph, which might advance my fame
So much as this poore song, which testifies
I did unto that day some sacrifice.

The one poem ties together a whole series of dualities. That Idios says he is "full of the common joy" can be interpreted to mean the joy common to all who went to that feast, or it can mean the joy common to all weddings regardless of special persons and circumstances. That he says the poem "was not made either the Court or mens hearts to invade" may mean that it was not designed for flattery but was rather sincere and genuine praise; or it may mean, since what is written is so obviously equivocal and halfhearted, that anyone can see that the poet would gain no entrance to the court by having written it. Therefore, that the epithalamium "might advance my fame" means that it might—or might not. But this is an easy game; the poem is ambiguous throughout. I cite one example from the epithalamium proper. After the bride has gone to bed, stanza 10 tells of "The Bridegroomes comming":

As he that sees a starre fall, runs apace,
    And findes a gellie in the place,
    So doth the Bridegroome hast as much,
Being told this starre is falne, and findes her such.

The word "gellie" means the meteorite, the common rock which the brilliant star is discovered to be when it has reached the end of its fall.[24] How could this fallen star fail

24. *Ibid.*, p. 97. Donne's "gellie" is not listed in the *Oxford English Dictionary*, but it seems to be related to "gell," of "unknown origin," according to the *O.E.D.*, and meaning "to ache

to suggest to anyone at court not only its coarse erotic meaning but also the unsavory character of the bride, her previous marriage, and the scandalous nullity suit just over? One needs to compare this wedding poem with the one Donne prepared for the Princess Elizabeth to see how he wrote when his heart was really in it.

Donne did write the poem. Nevertheless, the testimony, taken all together, shows clearly that he absented himself from the court on the day of the nuptials and that he did not complete his poem prior to the marriage nor indeed until sometime afterward. Its tone is so ambivalent, its insults so thinly veiled, that we must wonder, as Donne himself did, whether it helped or hindered him more at court.

It probably hindered him with Rochester. Though the then-reigning favorite apparently took Donne under his wing financially from the time of his first approach in 1612, Donne never was given any promise of court employment either as ambassador or as priest during the whole of Rochester's ascendancy. And it was not until near the close of 1614, when Rochester's own star was fading, that King James found the times right to see that Donne's shone more brightly. Donne's relationship with Rochester after the poem is indicated in an undated letter to "R. D." —probably Sir Robert Drury—"I cannot tell you so much, as you tell me, of anything from my Lord of Som[erset] since the epithalamium, for I heard nothing." [25]

I should myself wish to reverse Gosse's judgment on this epithalamium completely; it was written upon a razor's edge and, considered in its circumstances, was a brilliant success. By no means does it represent a slavish fawning

_____

or tingle with cold"; also to "gellid," meaning "cold as ice." All three seem to be cognates to the modern "jell," meaning "to harden when made cold."

25. Gosse, *Life*, II, 37.

upon a doubtful marriage in order to gain preferment, but neither is it a deliberate and foolhardy rejection of the possibility of that preferment. In the long run that marriage poem, with its ambiguities wreathed around it, made possible Donne's aim: to have his suit for preferment presented to the king.

But a problem remains yet about Donne's motivation for a vocation in the church. When he wrote that in seeking the profession of divinity he now obeyed "the inspirations (as I hope) of the Spirit of God," why did he add that parenthetical phrase? Is that not evidence enough of a doubt that he really was called by God to the priesthood and that until the very last he would not have become a clergyman if the king had not asked him to? Probably the answer to both questions is "yes," but neither affirmative means that he was insincere in his ordination. The mannerist concept will help us to see more particularly how Donne's doubtfulness toward a merely personal source for this resolution belonged to his vision of Christian faith. In a mannerist style of life the inner voice was not to be trusted as itself alone the voice of God; that pole needed to be confirmed by something from the outer world. And, as always for Donne, the outer world meant the court. Not until the king said, "I know Mr. Donne is a learned man, has the abilities of a learned divine, and will prove a powerful preacher; and my desire is to prefer him that way, and in that way I will deny you nothing for him," [26] did Donne feel that God had actually spoken to him, his voice being heard in the juncture of inner and outer.

By understanding Donne's call to the church in this way another puzzling fact can be resolved. In spite of the

26. Walton reports the words in his "The Life of Dr. John Donne," *Izaak Walton's "Lives,"* The Nelson Classics (London: Thomas Nelson & Sons, n.d.), p. 38. The speech is addressed to Rochester, probably "about the 20th of November, 1614," according to Gosse, *Life,* II, 59.

evidence of the letters which I have cited showing Donne himself first seeking the ministry, at a later time he claims the king made the first move. Gosse summarizes these claims, saying that Donne wrote, long afterward,

> "When I sit still and reckon all my old Master's royal favours to me, I return evermore to that—that he first inclined me to be a minister." And again, in the dedication of his *Devotions* of 1624 to Charles, Prince of Wales, he says: "In my second birth, your Highness's royal father vouchsafed me his hand, not only to sustain me in it, but to lead me to it." [27]

To these I add another from the *Devotions,* which Gosse (and Walton also) garbled. The *Devotions,* written during Donne's serious illness of 1623, here show him meditating on the king's having sent to him his own personal physician:

> But this his assisting to my bodily health, thou knowest, *O God,* and so doe some others of thine *honorable servants* know, is but the twy-light of that day, wherein thou, thorow him, hast shind upon mee before; but the *Eccho* of that voyce, whereby thou, through him, hast spoke to mee before; Then, when he, first of any man conceiv'd a hope, that I might be of some use in thy *Church,* and descended to an intimation, to a perswasion, almost to a solicitation, that I would embrace that calling. And thou who hadst put that desire into his heart, didst also put into mine, an obedience to it; and I who was sicke before, of a vertiginous giddines, and irresolution, and almost spent all my time in consulting how I should spend it, was by this *man of God,* and *God of men,* put into the poole, and recoverd.[28]

27. Gosse, *Life,* II, 60.
28. *Devotions Upon Emergent Occasions, by John Donne: Late Dean of Saint Paul's,* ed. John Sparrow (Cambridge, Eng.: At the University Press, 1923), p. 46. The *Devotions* were originally published in 1624.

"First of any man," Donne says of King James. But what of Donne himself? and what of Morton? Donne has told us the answer to these questions in this same passage: until he received the call from the authoritative voice in the outside world which matched the inner voice, he thought his own inclinations to be little more than chimeras, belonging to his characteristic "vertiginous giddiness and irresolution." Only then did irresolution turn to resolution; only when the king's spoken words entered Donne's ears and soul would he believe that any hope for his ordination had been genuinely conceived.

How worldly a man was John Donne? His inner life is judged primarily by our estimates of his poems, his outer primarily by his role as a churchman. The marriage between the two, achieved by a slow and circuitous movement, has been the subject of this book. Starting life as a Roman Catholic, Donne became an Anglican out of the challenges of the history of his own time, experienced in his psyche at considerable depth. In order finally to join the world as effectively as he could, he was ordained on January 23, 1615, by John King, the bishop of London. Shortly thereafter he was appointed to be reader of divinity to the benchers of Lincoln's Inn. Five years later King James made him dean of Saint Paul's, the post he held until his death in 1629. He never became a bishop, probably because he and Archbishop Abbot were too far separated in their religio-political vision; [29] but no evidence exists that

29. Gosse says of Abbot that he was "a very honest man" who was also "a primate of too great independence to please either James or his arrogant minions" (*Life,* II, 62). Gosse wanted to attribute Donne's never becoming bishop to his supposed nefarious role in the Rochester affair. It seems to me far more probable that Donne's attachment to the court rather than any specific misdeed is what led to his never securing sufficient favor from Abbot. Abbot was simply of the other party, the Puritan wing of the church, and under the growing tension of the times between Puritans and the more conservative court-oriented party, Donne

Donne ever wanted such a post. As dean of Saint Paul's he achieved something that was not in the archbishop's power to secure for him—the direct service to his king, in whose person church and state were joined. In the fulfillment of that aim, Donne rose higher than did the archbishop himself. In a certain way this aspect of the Anglican church was a survival of medieval feudalism; and Donne's kind of fulfillment was therefore soon to appear irrelevant to history. And yet it also partook of the new mannerist style, as that may be said to be illustrated in the new Jesuit Catholicism. To use language only a bit figuratively, it is fair to say that the king of England was John Donne's pope and that he himself was an Anglicized Jesuit.

The debate which rages between those who call Donne a "mystic" and those who deny it can be resolved only by those who can overcome their resistance to the irreconcilability of those poles. The combination of the mystical and the active life reappearing in recent history in the life of Dag Hammarskjöld,[30] for example, is by no means unique. It is one variant of a lengthy Western tradition. When Saint Thomas asked himself in the *Summa* whether the contemplative or the active was the better life, he replied that the contemplative was better but that it could not be achieved except when it was mixed with the active life.[31]

and Abbot were bound to appear out of each other's orbit. See my comments in Chap. IV, pp. 77–79.

30. For the mystical side see Hammarskjöld's *Markings,* translated from the Swedish by Leif Sjöberg and W. H. Auden (New York: Knopf, 1965).

31. Part II-II, Question 182: "Of the Active Life in Comparison with the Contemplative Life (*In Four Articles*)," in Saint Thomas Aquinas, *Summa Theologica,* first complete American edition, literally translated by Fathers of the English Dominican Province, 3 vols. (New York: Benziger Bros., 1947), II, 1942–46. Strictly speaking, Saint Thomas urges the superiority of the contemplative life, but he also urges with Gregory that one who would *"hold the fortress of contemplation, must first train in the camp of action"* (third article, p. 1945) and that the active life

Dag Hammarskjöld and Saint Thomas both lived the mixed life in a mode appropriate to their own times. So did John Donne. To do so was his vocation, and to discover this vocation in the mannerist mode meant that neither the inner nor the outer side of existence could be lightly treated; nor did Donne lightly treat them. He spent fourteen years resolving the vocational problem presented to him by his marriage, struggling with both the inner and outer worlds in the separated modes in which history and his own life presented them to him.

At no time in his life was John Donne merely "otherworldly," certainly not as Jack Donne, but not as Dean Donne either. However, neither would he settle for modernity's "worldliness," a notion which ought rather to be called "half-a-worldliness." Donne's achievement in joining the world meant also joining the halves; and in those terms he was as worldly a man as the history of his own life and times permitted him to be. The degree of his success made him one of the great exemplars of the mannerist life—perhaps, at least among literary figures, the greatest in England.

---

precedes the contemplative life (fourth article, pp. 1945–46). I am indebted to my friend, Professor James Case, of St. Michael's College, Winooski, Vermont, for identifying this passage in the *Summa*.

According to Keynes, Donne's ordinary motto, inscribed in his own handwriting on a large number of his personal books, is: *Per Rachel ho seruito, & non per Lea,* "I serve as Rachel did and not as Leah," i.e., in the contemplative rather than the active life. "This is a line from Petrarch (*Canz.* xix, st. 7, l. 1) and is founded on Gen. xxix. 25" (Geoffrey Keynes, *A Bibliography of Dr. John Donne,* 3d ed. [Cambridge: At the University Press, 1958], pp. 205–6).

CHAPTER VIII

DONNE'S SONNET
ON
CHRIST'S SPOUSE

Ever since its discovery and publication by Gosse in 1899 "Show me deare Christ" has been a crux in the understanding of Donne's religious life. Helen Gardner accords the problem a separate appendix, "The Interpretation of Donne's Sonnet on the Church," [1] which begins with a history of the dispute: Gosse, Grierson, and Bush each believe that the poem, presumed to have been written several years after he was ordained, shows the author still doubtful about the Anglican church; while Evelyn Simpson says that its views are "perfectly compatible with loyalty to the Church of England." Miss Gardner agrees with Mrs.

1. Helen Gardner, *John Donne: The Divine Poems* (Oxford: Oxford University Press, 1964), pp. 121–27. The quotations in the next two paragraphs are from these pages, except where I have indicated otherwise.

Simpson but says she would "put it more strongly. The subject of the sonnet is not 'Which is the best of existing Churches?'; but the contrast between the Church promised in Scripture and the Church as it appears in the world and throughout history."

Obviously this issue is meaningful only if the poem was written after Donne's ordination in 1615; for if it was written as early as 1609, when Miss Gardner dates the Divine Meditations, it would be perfectly natural to find Donne uncertain. The manuscript evidence for dating, however, which Miss Gardner used with such success for the Divine Meditations is of little help here. The principal fact is that this, together with two other sonnets, appears in a unique source, the Westmoreland Manuscript, and the three are usually dated by the one, "Since she whome I lov'd, hath payd her last debt," which concerns his wife's death and which therefore must have been written after that event in 1617. But no evidence compels us to believe that the other two were written at the same time; the Westmoreland Manuscript contains poems from many periods. In attempting to support a late dating, Miss Gardner comments that all three "are . . . quite distinct in their inspiration from the sixteen which precede them in the manuscript. They owe nothing in either subject or treatment to the tradition of formal meditation." [2] That comment seems to me to be true of all three except "Show me deare Christ," which contains as many of the marks of the formal meditation as do any of the sixteen Divine Meditations; note the impressive dramatic colloquy with which it begins. Miss Gardner further suggests that the reference to the church "which rob'd and tore / Laments and mournes in Germany" may allude to the "defeat of the Elector in the battle of the White Mountain, outside Prague, on 29 Octo-

2. *Ibid.,* p. xli.

ber 1620," but she does not urge this strongly, and it seems
the less likely because the church spoken about is not only
in Germany but "here." It could have been written, it seems
to me, as early as the other Divine Meditations and been
suppressed from circulation because of its content. But to
challenge the traditional dating on such a mere possibility
seems to me a doubtful procedure; furthermore, the inter-
pretation I shall be giving the poem tends to confirm the
later dating. So, even though the date of the poem remains
uncertain, I prefer to treat it here, at the conclusion to this
study of Donne's religious vocation.

To the extent that the poem is rightly considered a
"sonnet on the church," I agree with Miss Gardner and
Mrs. Simpson about Donne's churchmanship, and I should
like to give this position additional support, though calling
into question a few matters in Miss Gardner's way of
putting it. She strengthens her interpretation with a series
of identifications to the allusions in the poem, referring to
biblical sources on the one hand and to the history of
Donne's own times on the other. She concludes by review-
ing the war between Catholics and Protestants on the
visible and invisible churches, claiming that "Donne's state-
ment of the two opposite views, in the form of questions—
as if neither were tenable—is a sign of his sympathy with
the Anglican refusal to choose one of two mutually exclu-
sive positions." If this conclusion be taken to signify that
Donne has chosen a *via media* in which neither of the two
extremes is acceptable, then it ought to be corrected so that
we can see the possibility that he accepted both.

It is not often recognized that the Anglican *via media*
may just as well be understood to include as to exclude the
extremes of Rome and Geneva. The term *via media* is
founded on a geographical metaphor, in which the middle
way is said to be taken by those who walk the boundary
line between the two territories, as though that line were

itself a kind of neutral third territory belonging to neither of the other two. But one may also move along the same path by straddling the boundary, placing one foot first in the territory of one and the next in the territory of the other. In this style of walking, the person asserts that both countries belong to him to walk in, and his own special position is achieved through the third-dimensional *via media* created by his body as it moves along in the space above. It is this latter style of walking rather than the former which best describes Donne's Anglicanism; it is precisely what I described in an earlier chapter under the label of mannerism.

Into this context I would place the well-known statement of 1609 describing his religious position:

> You know I never fettered nor imprisoned the word Religion, not straightening it friarly, *ad Religiones factitas* (as the Romans call well their orders of Religion), nor immuring it in a Rome, or a Wittemberg, or a Geneva; they are all virtual beams of one Sun, and wheresoever they find clay hearts, they harden them and moulder them into dust; and they entender and mollify waxen. They are not so contrary as the North and South Poles, and that [?] they are co-natural pieces of one circle. Religion is Christianity, which being too spiritual to be seen by us, doth therefore take an apparent body of good life and works, so salvation requires an honest Christian.[3]

The sun, standing above the rays it sheds on "a Rome, or a Wittemberg, or a Geneva," is a better figure of speech, he says, than the body of the world between a North and South Pole for representing that commendable "Christian-

3. Gosse, *Life,* I, 226. "A letter to Sir H. R.," as Gosse prints it, but probably to Sir Henry Goodyer, according to Herbert J. C. Grierson, *The Poems of John Donne,* 2 vols. (Oxford: Oxford University Press, 1912), II, 115, who cites it in connection with the third Satire.

ity . . . too spiritual to be seen by us" (he does not
mention "a Canterbury").

But how are the contrasting "territories" presented in the
poem? They are given to us in a whole series of questions
which occupy the second through the tenth lines. Each of
them is a response to the opening demand:

> Show me deare Christ, thy spouse, so bright and cleare.
> What, is it she, which on the other shore
> Goes richly painted? or which rob'd and tore
> Laments and mournes in Germany and here?
> Sleepes she a thousand, then peepes up one yeare?
> Is she selfe truth and errs? now new, now outwore?
> Doth she,'and did she, and shall she evermore
> On one, or seaven, or on no hill appeare?
> Dwells she with us, or like adventuring knights
> First travaile we to seeke and then make love? [4]

A series of choices seems to be presented between pairs of
alternatives (except in lines 7 and 8, where a choice of
three is given). But are these alternatives really stated "as if
neither were tenable"? Certainly the poem may be read
that way, as if, for example, the spouse could certainly not
be a whore or a raped woman. But it is equally clear that
she might be both, and this is the reconciliation suggested
in the final couplet, where she is

> most trew, and pleasing to thee, then
> When she'is embrac'd and open to most men.

But this is not clear to us upon first entering the poem;
any certainty about the answers is precluded by the poet's
giving us the identity of the spouse only in the form of
questions. And if we are mentally replying to those ques-
tions "No, certainly not, it could not be she, nor she," we

4. Gardner, *John Donne: The Divine Poems,* p. 15. I have
used Gardner's text of this poem throughout this chapter.

must be aware that we could equally well be replying "Yes, no doubt it might be she, or she." Yet, on the other hand, programmatic uncertainty is undercut by the fact that the possibility of discovering some kind of definite answer also lies implicit in the very asking of the questions. Consequently, the questions seem to express a dialectic of doubt and confidence, or skepticism and faith, and Donne to embrace both. If we were to ask if it is possible for anyone to have such contrary religious attitudes, the answer would have to be "Yes, of course, since he has done it," even if the reader of this book were not familiar by now with the simultaneous embracing of contrary views, and even if doing so were not a perfectly conventional religious position known during that period as fideism. The most familiar expositor of that position to students of English literature is Sir Thomas Browne in the *Religio Medici*, who says, for example,

> I am confident and fully persuaded, yet dare not take my oath of my salvation; I am as it were sure, and do believe, without all doubt, that there is such a city as *Constantinople*; yet for me to take my oath thereon, were a kinde of perjury, because I hold no infallible warrant from my owne sense, to confirme me in the certainty thereof.[5]

He is both certain and doubtful of his salvation, and that is natural enough, since "faith," to have any genuine reality, must be the result of something not ascertainable. Thus he says also that, "since I was of understanding to know we know nothing, my reason hath beene more pliable to the will of faith." [6]

What does this mean for Donne's Anglicanism? It means that we cannot give this poem a reading which will

---

5. *Religio Medici*, Pt. I, sec. 59, in *The Works of Sir Thomas Browne*, ed. Geoffrey Keynes (Chicago: University of Chicago Press, 1964), I, 68.
6. Pt. I, sec. 10 (*ibid.*, p. 19).

clearly exculpate Donne from the charge of uncertainty about the Anglican church, nor should we; for a man of the middle way is not properly "certain," in the sense in which his way is correct over against other ways which are incorrect. The Anglican tone is well expressed by the title chosen by William Chillingworth for his polemical defense against Rome, *The Religion of Protestants a Safe Way to Salvation* (1637). "Certainty of salvation" was the characteristic language of one wing of Calvinists, which also had an equivalent in Catholicism; but one who embraced both such extremes hardly achieves the kind of certainty that one or the others of these may. However, he can, out of his very doubtfulness, achieve his own individual kind of confidence, the confidence that doubt is itself the vehicle of salvation. The fear generated by the uncertainty of choice between Rome and Geneva provides the energy necessary to propel him across the trackless dark between these extremes. "And truely," says Browne, expressing something of the assurance which may come to those who live in such doubt, "though many pretend an absolute certainty of their salvation, yet when an humble soule shall contemplate her owne unworthinesse, she shall meete with many doubts and suddainely finde how much we stand in need of the Precept of Saint *Paul, Worke out your salvation with feare and trembling.*" [7] The very uncertainties in the poem which give rise to the charges of insincerity against Donne actually support the assertion of his essential Anglicanism.

Achieving resolution through irresolution, faith through doubt, certainty through uncertainty, was an awkward, wobbling movement of the soul, but, by it, Donne and the others he shared it with could join into one, at least for a time, two territories which must otherwise have fallen into irreconcilable hostilities—and which, in somewhat transferred form, very shortly did. The joining was achieved

7. Pt. I, sec. 59 (*ibid.,* p. 68).

fundamentally by the inner experience of an individual man. Yet the inner experience had to have its outward expression, as Donne knew as early as the writing of the third Satire. If he had been a Frenchman, that form might have been the Gallican wing of Roman Catholicism; had he been Dutch, he might have been an Arminian Calvinist or a Jansenist Catholic; but he was an Englishman, and so he became an Anglican. In order to join Rome and Geneva properly, one might have his head in the skies—even as high as the sun—but he must have his feet on the ground.

Here I might leave the discussion of the poem. To be sure, I have said hardly a word about the last four lines, but they are very difficult. I have treated the issue which has been conventionally raised; and having now saved Donne, I could save myself. Unfortunately, hinging the interpretation of the poem solely upon this issue has the effect of leaving the most important things about the poem unsaid, and the attitude which produces this result is summarized and made almost inevitable when we permit the subject of the poem to be called the "church." In a broader sense we are led astray whenever we permit ourselves to be exclusively tied to the "critical" tradition in scholarship, whether that be the "critical-historical" variant or the "critical-aesthetic." This tradition has its roots in the effort to find all meaning within the realm of the intellect; it has its greatest metaphysical support probably in Kant's *Critiques*, from which the term "critical" and the attitude which accompanies it have gained their large following. Among Kant's writings we should not be surprised to find a work entitled *Religion within the Limits of Reason Alone.*[8] But as we

8. See A. C. Ewing, *A Short Commentary on Kant's "Critique of Pure Reason"* (London: Methuen, 1938), for a helpful treatment of the critical attitude, especially Chapter III, "The Transcendental Deduction of the Categories," and the opening pages of Chapter V, "Kant's Attitude to Material Idealism. The Thing-in-Itself."

have already observed, neither Donne's poetry nor his religion is the outcome of reason alone, and we certainly should not expect this of his religious poetry. "Show me deare Christ" is the outcome, like the other religious poems, of passionate intellect, and that is what is meant by calling them "spiritual."

The poem should be referred to as Donne's "Sonnet on Christ's spouse." "Christ's spouse" is Donne's own language; nowhere does he use the antiseptic term "church." Of course the spouse of Christ is one of the figures by which the church is traditionally represented, but when the word "church" is used in contemporary scholarly communication, the spouse of Christ is seldom the understanding it receives; or if it is said to be such in a bare word or phrase, what does that signify, save that one has given a perfectly knowable institution an obscurantist and obsolete label? Donne's figure of the "spouse" has its roots in the language of Scripture, and it is there that we must turn for the spiritual meaning of the poem. It is in these terms, as they stamped themselves upon his psyche through reading (and liturgical and other experiences), that we will discover the inner life of the poet and whatever bearing it might have on our estimate of his outer life, including his "church," insofar as that term can still be apprehended in some genuine way.

What, then, does the poem allude to from Scripture? Miss Gardner finds the "spouse, so bright and cleare" in Revelation 19:7-8, [9] where in preparing for the "marriage

9. All biblical quotations in this chapter are from the Revised Standard Version. According to Potter and Simpson, Donne himself seems usually to have used the Vulgate, the Geneva, and the Authorized Version. He quoted in English, either from his own translation of the Vulgate, or sometimes the Hebrew, or freely from memory of the English versions. "In his *Essays in Divinity* Donne used the Geneva Bible throughout," and he seemed to have preferred the Geneva version before he became dean of

of the Lamb" we read that "his Bride has made herself
ready; it was granted her to be clothed with fine linen,
bright and pure." Where the bride is alluded to under the
figure of the "mild dove," Miss Gardner finds her in the
Song of Solomon 5:2, "Open to me, my sister, my love, my
dove, my perfect one." The woman who in the sonnet "goes
richly painted" she identifies with the "Babylonish woman"
(Miss Gardner's phrase) of Revelation 17:4, who is "ar-
rayed in purple and scarlet, and bedecked with gold and
jewels and pearls, holding in her hand a golden cup full of
abominations and the impurities of her fornication" and
said in the verse following to have written on her head "a
name of mystery: 'Babylon the great, mother of harlots and
of earth's abominations.' " Donne's woman "rob'd and
tore" Miss Gardner finds in the image of Jerusalem de-
scribed in Lamentations 2:5, "The Lord has become like an
enemy, he has destroyed Israel, he has destroyed all its
palaces, laid in ruins its strongholds; and he has multiplied
in the daughter of Judah mourning and lamentation," and
2:13, "What can I say for you, to what compare you, O
daughter of Jerusalem? What can I liken to you, that I
may comfort you, O virgin daughter of Zion? For vast as
the sea is your ruin; who can restore you?" [10]

But such precise identifications fail to note that the figure
of the spouse, in both her loyal and disloyal relationships to
her husband, pervades great stretches of the Bible and is
indeed one of the keys to unlocking its over-all unity and
meaning. The pervasiveness of the marital imagery of the
Bible would have been a commonplace for Donne, however

Saint Paul's (*The Sermons of John Donne,* ed. Evelyn M. Simp-
son and George Potter, 10 vols. [Berkeley and Los Angeles: Uni-
versity of California Press, 1962], X, 306–28; the sentence
quoted here is from p. 325).

10. Where Miss Gardner has herself quoted the biblical pas-
sages she uses the King James Version.

veiled it has become for us; and we cannot enter the spiritual dimension in the poem without discovering how this metaphor works in the over-all movement of biblical history and meaning.

The "spouse" of the New Testament has its origin in the Old Testament, where, in spite of the apparent sexual contradictions, her beginning is in the patriarch Jacob, renamed "Israel" after his night of wrestling with God. Israel inherits the promises in the covenant, originally made by God with Abraham, one of which was that his descendants should be numbered as the sands of the sea, or the stars of the sky, or the dust of the earth, as it appears in one or another of several variants. When these offspring have multiplied into the twelve sons and the twelve tribes who are their offspring in turn, they are known collectively by the name of "Israel" as well as by the phrase "children of Israel," so that the one name "Israel" signifies both the patriarch and the total community. This identity of the single man with the community is what H. Wheeler Robinson calls Israel's "corporate personality." [11] This usage is not a mere convention, as it might appear: the children of Israel are understood to be the exfoliation of the original seed in the loins of the one man, Jacob-Israel; hence his offspring are him (or a part of him) in a literal biological sense; they are his seed; they are, hence, his actual corpus, or bodily person, in what it has later become. Because of this literal biological identity, it is odd to consider the corporate personality of "Israel" to be a mere "personification," as though we dealt here only with a figure of speech, a metaphor. The covenant, which expresses the relationship between Yahweh and the corporate personality of Israel,

11. H. Wheeler Robinson, *Inspiration and Revelation in the Old Testament* (Oxford: Oxford University Press, 1946), pp. 70 ff.

after appearing at first as Yahweh's promises only, later takes on the familiar contractual aspects in which Israel owes the Lord obedience to his commandments in return for his leadership and concern over them.

Although in the earlier books of the Old Testament, those that tend to be received by us as historical, Israel appears exclusively in the male gender, a curious thing happens in the prophetic (or poetic) books: we now frequently hear of the "daughters of Israel," and simultaneously a female Israel appears who is married to Yahweh. The name is not always "Israel"; sometimes it is "Judah," reflecting the situation in which the kingdom once unified under David had split into a northern and a southern kingdom, Israel and Judah, with Judah being the dominant partner. Or sometimes the reference is to the "daughters of Zion" or "Zion," or the "daughters of Jerusalem" or "Jerusalem," these two being practical equivalents, since Jerusalem was built on Mount Zion. This female figure, her birth and development culminating in the marriage with Yahweh, is described by the Lord in Ezekiel 16:3–8:

> Your origin and your birth are of the land of the Canaanites; your father was an Amorite, and your mother a Hittite. And as for your birth, on the day you were born your navel string was not cut, nor were you washed . . . but you were cast out on the open field, for you were abhorred, on the day that you were born. And when I passed by you, and saw you weltering in your blood, I said to you in your blood, "Live, and grow up like a plant of the field." And you grew up and became tall and arrived at full maidenhood; your breasts were formed, and your hair had grown; yet you were naked and bare. When I passed by you again and looked upon you, behold, you were at the age for love; and I spread my skirt over you, and covered your nakedness: yea, I plighted my troth to you and entered into a covenant with you, says the Lord GOD, and you became mine.

The marriage was not a happy one, because the bride was disloyal to her husband, as the prophets repeat again and again, calling her a faithless and errant whore for her continual adulteries with other lovers. The other lovers are, of course, other divinities: Ashteroth or Dagon, for example, or more often the Baals who were worshiped by the Canaanites. Adultery in the prophets, therefore, signifies idolatry, the two concepts being fused into one, as may be illustrated in some verses in Ezekiel 16, following shortly after those quoted above:

> But you trusted in your beauty, and played the harlot because of your renown, and lavished your harlotries on any passer-by. You took some of your garments, and made for yourself gaily decked shrines, and on them played the harlot; the like has never been, nor ever shall be. You also took your fair jewels of my gold and of my silver, which I had given you, and made for yourself images of men, and with them played the harlot.

Israel the harlot appears briefly in Amos; she is more important in Isaiah; several powerful passages in Jeremiah and Ezekiel describe and denounce her and her ways; and she dominates the whole of Hosea. Hosea marries the prostitute, Gomer, in order to create a living parable of the Lord's faithfulness to his faithless bride, for he, in spite of Israel's repeated adulteries—though he will cajole, denounce, threaten, or punish her—will not forsake her. The Lord lives in the promise of a future day when she will be again "as in the days of her youth, and as at the time when she came out of the land of Egypt. And in that day, says the LORD, you will call me, 'My husband,' and no longer will you call me, 'My Ba'al' " (Hosea 2:15–16).[12]

12. "Ba'al" means "Lord" or "Master," as is explained in a footnote on this passage in *The Oxford Bible*, ed. Herbert G. May and Bruce M. Metzger (New York: Oxford University Press, 1965), p. 1090.

In that day she shall say, "I will go and return to my first husband, for it was better with me then than now" (Hosea 2:7).

C. G. Jung's typology of the animus and the anima, mentioned above, showing that the gender of the soul side of a person is the reverse of his body type, can help us to grasp why Israel's gender switches from male to female when we move from the historical to the prophetic books. The figure is male in the historical books, because there the external image of Israel is spoken about, and female (often) in the other, because there the inner image of Israel is represented. The novelty of speaking this way, if it is novel, is abated somewhat when we realize that talking about the inner image of Israel is little more than another way of saying something quite conventional, namely, that the prophetic and poetic books are the so-called "spiritual" books of the Old Testament. They represent the transformation of the earlier external religion into a "spiritual" religion.

The momentous event which produced this transformation was the Babylonian captivity, in which the nation of Israel, the holy city Jerusalem, and the temple and its worship were all destroyed. After that, when the principal events of the history of Israel are heard of again—the Creation, the Egyptian slavery, the Red Sea, the wilderness, the stone tablets, etc.—they appear as memories. They are now aspects of Israel's psychic life. Hence, for example, after the temple is destroyed in the Babylonian conquest, the ritual sacrifices of the temple worship are transformed into spiritual sacrifice: "The sacrifice acceptable to God is a broken spirit; a broken and a contrite heart, O God, thou wilt not despise." [13] Jeremiah is usually said to have founded the spiritual religion in an important passage an-

13. Psalm 51; but the same meaning occurs in Amos 5:21–24, Isaiah 1:11–17, Micah 6:6–8, and Jeremiah 7:4–7.

nouncing a "new covenant," which is to replace the old and in which the metaphor of Yahweh as the husband of Israel also appears:

> Behold, the days are coming, says the LORD, when I will make a new covenant with the house of Israel and the house of Judah, not like the covenant which I made with their fathers when I took them by the hand to bring them out of the land of Egypt, my covenant which they broke, though I was their husband, says the LORD. But this is the covenant which I will make with the house of Israel after those days. Says the LORD: I will put my law within them, and I will write it upon their hearts; and I will be their God, and they shall be my people.
>
> (Jer. 31:31–33)

By coming to the Song of Solomon against the background of this new spiritual religion we best appreciate the so-called "allegorical" interpretation of that book. Who, for example, can the female lover of Chapter 4 be but Israel, whose very landscape provides the similes by which her beauty is described?

> Behold, you are beautiful, my love,
>   behold, you are beautiful!
> Your eyes are doves
>   behind your veil.
> Your hair is like a flock of goats,
>   moving down the slopes of Gilead.
> Your teeth are like a flock of shorn ewes
>   that have come up from the washing,
> all of which bear twins,
>   and not one among them is bereaved.
> Your lips are like a scarlet thread,
>   and your mouth is lovely.
> Your cheeks are like halves of a pomegranate
>   behind your veil.
> Your neck is like the tower of David,
>   built for an arsenal,

whereon hang a thousand bucklers,
    all of them shields of warriors.
Your two breasts are like two fawns,
    twins of a gazelle,
      that feed among the lilies.

                    (Song of Sol. 4:1–5)

Of course, most of these similes might allude to any pastoral geography, but the "tower of David" clearly specifies the territory of Israel. And who is the shepherd-king husband of Chapters 3 and 5 but Yahweh, whose identity is revealed by his mysterious invisibility at the very moment when his presence is most deeply felt and desired?

My beloved put his hand to the latch,
    and my heart was thrilled within me.
I arose to open to my beloved,
    and my hands dripped with myrrh,
My fingers with liquid myrrh,
    upon the handles of the bolt.
I opened to my beloved,
    but my beloved had turned and gone.
My soul failed me when he spoke.
I sought him, but found him not;
    I called him, but he gave no answer.

                    (Song of Sol. 5:4–6)

With all of this Old Testament preparation we wonder the less when the new covenant Jeremiah announced is realized by the consummation of the marriage in the New Testament and its fruition in the birth of a son. The New Testament of course is not merely a description of "facts" but is a transfigured description, the "facts" as they were received and felt by the writers, all members presumably of that new community of early Christians. This transfiguration renewed many of the archetypes of the Old Testament, the best known of which is probably the messiah (or king) but the most important of which, for our purposes, is the marriage. The community of the church is now the bride carrying on the tradition of the female Israel, and Christ, who is the New Testament transfiguration of the Lord, carries on the tradition of the divine husband. Like Israel in the Old Testament, the church has both a male and female identity, female as the bride of Christ and male as the body of Christ.

So much for the true bride. But what of that whore Israel? It is important for understanding "Show me deare Christ" to realize that the bride does not appear as a whore anywhere in the New Testament. The whore of the book of Revelation, cited by Miss Gardner, is the whore *of Babylon,* adumbrated in Isaiah 47:1 ff., not Israel the whore; and this whore of Babylon is never even a candidate for the Lord's bride in the Old or the New Testaments. In the New Testament she is a figure symbolizing those persons at the end of time who have not become part of the true Israel and who are irredeemably faithless and lost.

Because of the vast involvement of both the Old and New Testaments in the marital metaphor, the figure (or figures) Donne alludes to in his poem can be identified, not once or a few times only, but many many times. Donne's "she, which on the other shore goes richly painted" should not be identified with the whore of Babylon, since in the final lines of the poem she and the spouse are the same. But she can be identified with Hosea's wife, Gomer, who "decked herself with her rings and jewelry and went after her lovers, and forgot me, says the LORD" (Hos. 2:13). Since Gomer is not specifically said to be "painted," perhaps Jeremiah's whore provides a better parallel, about whom the Lord says: "What do you mean that you dress in scarlet, that you deck yourself with ornaments of gold, that you enlarge your eyes with paint?" (Jer. 4:30), or Ezekiel's, who is derided by the Lord, because for other gods "you bathed yourself, painted your eyes, and decked yourself with ornaments" (Ezek. 23:40).

Although the woman who "rob'd and tore laments and mourns" can be well identified only in the figure of Jerusalem (alias Zion, or the daughters of Zion, or the daughters of Judah) in the Book of Lamentations, where Miss Gardner found her, the verbal parallels as well as the over-all picture can best be seen by quoting from several verses:

> She weeps bitterly in the night, tears on her cheeks; among all her lovers she has none to comfort her . . . Jerusalem sinned grievously, therefore she became filthy; all who honoured her despise her, for they have seen her nakedness. . . . Her uncleanness was in her skirts. . . . He has multiplied in the daughter of Judah mourning and lamentation. . . . The elders of the daughter of Zion . . . have cast dust on their heads and put on sackcloth; the maidens of Jerusalem have bowed their heads to the ground.
>
> (Lam. 1 and 2 passim)

While Donne's spouse "so bright and cleare" is obviously a New Testament figure, it is wrong simply to identify her with the bride of the Book of Revelation, where she is presented wholly without spot or stain. Her Old Testament lineage reveals better the character Donne gives her. The description of the bride's clothing in Revelation, "of fine linen, clean and white," almost certainly depends upon certain similar words in the much fuller description in Ezekiel 16, following the betrothal scene quoted above:

> I clothed you also with embroidered cloth and shod you with leather, I swathed you in fine linen and covered you with silk. And I decked you with ornaments, and put bracelets on your arms, and a chain on your neck. And I put a ring on your nose, and earrings in your ears, and a beautiful crown upon your head. Thus you were decked with gold and silver; and your raiment was of fine linen,

and silk, and embroidered cloth; you ate fine flour and honey and oil. You grew exceedingly beautiful, and came to regal estate. And your renown went forth among the nations because of your beauty, for it was perfect through the splendor which I had bestowed upon you.

(Ezek. 16:10–14)

Language close to Donne's "bright and cleare" can also be found in the Song of Solomon, where the spouse is said to be "fair as the moon, bright as the sun" (6:10), a passage in which she is also alluded to as a "dove," as Donne did in line 12 of the sonnet.

The Song of Solomon is more significant for "Show me deare Christ" and for Donne's other "love of God" sonnets than simple verbal parallels permit us to see, and we can grasp that significance better, now that we have seen how the divine marriage appears elsewhere in biblical literature. The "love of God" sonnets, all except "Show me deare Christ," show the female soul lost and wandering, looking for an absent Lord-lover. This was the basic situation described in my retelling of the myth-narrative implicit in the poems in Chapter VI; and it originates of course in the Song of Solomon, though it came to Donne through many intermediaries.[14] "Show me deare Christ" is a much more

14. See Stanley Stewart, *The Enclosed Garden: The Tradition and the Image in Seventeenth-Century Poetry* (Madison: University of Wisconsin Press, 1966), especially the section on the "Spiritual Marriage," in which he presents an analysis of "Show me deare Christ" that is in some important respects similar to my own (pp. 19–22). I would have made more use of Stewart's book had it not come to my attention too late. I consider my own treatment of the poem more thorough than Stewart's, and of course I have shown its relation to Donne's biography, which he has not. On the other hand, Stewart's treatment shows more deeply the connection of the spouse imagery to the mystical and medieval intermediaries through which the traditions of the divine marriage must have reached Donne. I consider his interpretation wrong, or at best only half-right, when he alludes approvingly to Miss Gardner's identification of the spouse with the bride of the Apocalypse and says, of the line "let myne amor-

complex poem than any of these, and one aspect of this complexity is discovered in the fact that here it is the spouse rather than the husband who is missing from view, a matter whose significance I cannot make clear immediately but which is connected with the fact that this poem celebrates the consummation of the marriage only longed for in the earlier poems. The union is represented only in the last four lines of the poem, in which the tension set up in the first ten is resolved:

11 Betray kind husband thy spouse to our sights,
12 And let myne amorous soule court thy mild Dove,
13 Who is most trew, and pleasing to thee, then
14 When she'is embrac'd and open to most men.

The last two lines reconcile the image of the true with the false bride, thereby simultaneously reconcilling the fallen churches to the one true church and multiplicity with unity. But lines 11 and 12 also admit "myne amorous soule" into the courtship, and this adds the poet himself into the reconciliatory pattern.

But precisely how do the allusions and references in the last lines work? Considerable confusion emerges if one tries to follow these out individually. Is the spouse "thy mild Dove," for example? It is the most natural reading syntactically: "Who" in line 13 refers to the noun nearest it (the "Dove"), while "myne amorous soule" emerges as a male lover competitive with Christ for the love of the spouse.

---

ous soule court thy mild Dove," that "all souls must remain in an anxious state, to one degree or another, until the final wedding in the New Jerusalem" (p. 21) since, as Stewart himself also said elsewhere, the poem celebrates the wedding of the soul to Christ and of man to the external church. But I find him importantly right when he asserts that "the speaker is himself the Bride of Christ" (p. 20), a reading which does not prevent the Bride of Christ also from alluding to the external church. He does not show that the speaker also is Christ—but he is; in the fullest sense of the mystical union, all opposites are joined and become one.

This reading fulfills nicely the implications of the whore-spouse of the last line. But does the speaker play no part in this union? Is he merely to be identified with his "amorous soule?" Could it be that "she" is the invisible speaker himself?

If "she" is identified as the speaker, one could justify the difficulty he (now "she") has had in seeing her earlier in the poem; he has been looking everywhere except at himself. The speaker's shift in tone gradually reveals his feminine character: He begins the poem with a demand, "show me," modulates with the word "betray," and concludes with the request "let." Thus, the speaker identifies himself with "thy mild dove," and since "myne amorous soule" is also obviously an aspect of the speaker's total person, the marriage is seen as an inner union, a sense of reconciliation of the male and female aspects of the speaker's own self. The marriage becomes the joining of Christ to the invisible church. Yet the final lines clearly imply the speaker's accepting the role of joining an external church, a fallen bride who is "out there" in history—and this identification seems to ignore that.[15]

15. Or could she be identified with "myne amorous soule"? This reading has the advantage of giving the dove a male gender, as it has in the New Testament: the Holy Spirit is said to descend at the time of Jesus' baptism "like a dove" (Mark 1:10, John 1:32, Luke 3:22, Matt. 3:16), and this dove is traditionally identified with the divine husband of the Virgin Mary. Even in the Song of Solomon—where, to be sure, the dove appears twice in the female gender (5:2 and 6:9)—it appears also once as the male lover (2:14), and, of three occurrences of "dove's eyes," two are of the male lover (1:15 and 5:12).

But it would make "myne amorous soule" female, which (though it is the way the soul appears in the other "love of God" sonnets) implies that Donne's spouse is only to be the spiritual church. But the poem wants to resolve the problem of the external church, and how can she, as the "amorous soule," do that? She can—in a sort of a way. Reading "myne amorous soule" as the spouse, it is she "who" in line 12 is "most trew" to her husband (the "mild Dove"), when in the final lines she (still the spiritual church) is able to receive "most men," that is, when

Treating her as having one or another identity in this way has the effect of revealing diverse and multiple meanings, together with doubts and problems. This does not mean that it is wrong to do so; it is one right way, but there is another: to treat the marital metaphor as central and to accept its implication that things which seem diverse and even inconsistent are also one and the same. Male and female join in marriage, the "two being one are it," as Donne had said of the lovers in "The Canonization," where it was, however, a simple description, while here the union is a poetic effect in which the separate identity of this or that word or meaning is dissolved. A poetic effect close to the one achieved in "Show me deare Christ" can be seen in the second stanza of "A Valediction: of Weeping," where almost all the distinguishable meanings in the poem are merged or lost when the "nothing" of stanza 1 becomes the "all" of stanza 2. This merging is climaxed poetically in the lines where "thy tears mixt with mine doe overflow / This world, by waters sent from thee, my heaven dissolved so." Thus the "waters sent from thee," for instance, may be seen as her tears or his tears (caused by her), a sample only of identifications so multiple that not only "my heaven" but the whole world of meaning is threatened with dissolution.

The resolution of "Show me, deare Christ" by its high degree of metaphoric complexity also produces a merging of meanings so that precise identification becomes a game of limited value; and what that suggests, of course, is that here we have an aesthetic model of the consummation

---

she is married to an external church composed of the largest possible number of individual churches or sects. The external church is now revealed in the male figure rather than the female, the body of Christ rather than his bride. "She" can't be seen because she is invisible, and she becomes the true church only when she is united to the visible historical figure. But this reading makes the syntax difficult; and, worse yet, it stumbles over the word "court," for it is the male, not the female, lover who generally courts.

itself. That seems to become possible at the moment we are given permission to shift our attention from an apparently exclusive focus on the world outside the poet toward his own individual self (especially his inner self), understood, however, in such a way as metaphorically to allude also to that outer world. Once this is seen, it is possible to go back to the beginning and reread the entire poem in the light of the resolution.

Suppose we begin by giving the resolved identity to the figure of Christ. We know from the most natural reading of the final line that Christ merges with the speaker's "amorous soule" (since the soul acts in Christ's role as husband). Even without the final lines, a clue to the inner presence of Christ is adumbrated in the ease with which the speaker addresses him—as though there, in his very presence. That mode of address is, of course, structured on the model of the colloquy of the meditative tradition, where the figure spoken to is recreated imaginatively (after one has read, or recalled having heard, some part of the Gospel story). What is actually being represented in the poem then, is an internal dialogue in which "Christ" is a figure representing a presence within, the image of the divine immanence, or, approximately, one's own psyche, the awareness of life within insofar as that is contiguous with life or the source of life outside oneself. This awareness of the divine immanence has not disappeared from Western consciousness since the decline of the public use of Christian symbols, but it has generally emerged since then in light or vegetation imagery or, in no sensory imagery at all, as an abstraction, power, the unknown, or the like. But for Donne to perceive the divine immanence in the image of a person, specifically Christ, merely meant to participate in a long tradition which he would have been perfectly familiar with. At least from the time of the development of Logos Christology, the Jesus born in the flesh in Bethlehem was

understood to be the Word (or Logos) who was "begotten
of his Father before all worlds" and "by whom all things
were made" (to quote the formulations made conventional
in the Nicene Creed). Hence the Logos is the figure, or
archetype, of generation itself. Whether or not one discov-
ered that creative principle within one's own life depended
upon whether one had received it by faith and was oneself
regenerated by that power. If so, the "everlasting life" with
which one's own life is now identified one perceives in the
name and identity of "Christ."

To this generative archetype, then, the speaker begins to
speak in the words "Show me deare Christ," aware of him
more as the divine immanence the more he seems to be a
person within himself. Of this Christ, the speaker requests
to be shown the bride "bright and cleare." At the moment,
it is hidden from the speaker that he himself (who is the
little world of the external church, or its corporate person)
could be the bride. Were this to be immediately apparent,
the resolution would be too rapid and the poem too thin.
The speaker ignores himself tentatively and presents in-
stead an intervening set of questions enlarging the vision
outside himself in which the spouse might be embodied. Of
these, the whore and the raped woman are the closest to the
metaphor of the marriage, each being clearly the figure of a
woman. But is either the spouse? And, if so, is either one
the spouse "so bright and cleare"? Knowing the Scriptural
background, we know that in some sense the whore *is* also
the true bride. But her appearance has been changed. Her
original innocent nakedness had been covered with gar-
ments of fine linen by her husband-lover, the Lord, which
she has now, in order to play him false, exchanged for
gaudy clothes and a painted face. The woman who "rob'd
and tore laments and mournes in Germany and here" is
also the true spouse, as she appears in Lamentations, when
she is in captivity after the Babylonian conquest. The sexual

and marital imagery is abated for several lines following, and returns again in lines 9 and 10:

> Dwells she with us, or like adventuring knights
> First travaile we to seeke and then make love? [16]

"Dwells she with us," in this reading, now looks ahead to the resolution in Donne's own person to be made in the concluding lines, contrasted with the remainder, which looks back at the search in the external world.

To look merely at the outward show of things, though this is not adequate for the full disclosure, has a function in the search. Being thwarted or baffled there, the speaker is driven to search elsewhere. But where? Perhaps we are to construe the seeing of the bride (at least in this kind of inner interpretation) in quite a different way. Perhaps we are to understand her as fully disclosed to our sight only

---

16. Miss Gardner comments on these two lines: "Two conceptions of the Church are given here in terms of two conceptions of love—the domestic and the romantic. Donne had not much sympathy with the latter; and allusions to medieval romance are very rare in his poetry" (*The Divine Poems,* p. 80). But Donne had a sympathy for both. To be sure, once married, Donne lived a regular and domestic life with his wife. But does not his secret courtship and marriage, "the great mistake of his life," as the domestically minded Walton called it, suggest some of the elements of romance? As usual, Donne wants to have it both ways: clandestine, imprudent, offensive at first; but, having done it that way, he does not rest satisfied until he has had his love affair the other way also, including a proper and legal Christian marriage ceremony followed by patient years of waiting upon his father-in-law's change of heart. That Donne seldom alludes to medieval romance in his poetry is of little effect. Such an allusion appears here and again in the word "court" in line 12. If the romantic search in the poem appears to be for the spouse of Christ rather than for some other female, is this not good evidence that she now happens to be the form into which Donne is translating the traditional romantic love affair, adultery and all? Miss Gardner also finds in the pilgrimage implicit in these lines an image of the New Jerusalem, that is, the bride of the Apocalypse, who is accessible only at the very end of this time and space; but such a reading seems to me inconsistent with the imagery of the final line, as I have indicated in the text.

when she can be seen unclothed, in which her nakedness is
the figure for the individual man rather than the corporate
whole or, on another level, for the soul rather than the
body of the church.[17] A revelation of nakedness is implied
by the opening word of line 11:

> Betray kind husband thy spouse to our sights.

The psychological implications of this switch from the
innocent "show" of line 1 already suggest the meaning to
be brought out more clearly in the final line. The "be-
trayal" involved in showing off one's wife in this way is
well illustrated by the story Herodotus tells of Gyges.[18] A
certain king Candaules had a beautiful wife, of whom he
was inordinately proud. Wanting to impress his friend
Gyges, Candaules arranged to have her unveiled in such a
way that she was unaware of being seen. But the queen
discerned what had happened and was so angry at this that
she invited Gyges to kill her husband and become king or
suffer the consequence of being killed himself. Gyges chose
life, killed Candaules, and become the husband of the beau-
tiful woman and king of the realm.

Because of the betrayal one important way of resolving

---

17. Compare Richard Crashaw's "Hymn to St. Teresa," where
the "spouse" (Christ) urges her back from her planned martyr-
dom among the Moors:

> Blest powres forbid, Thy tender life
> Should bleed upon a barborous knife;
> Or some base hand have power to race
> Thy Brest's chast cabinet, and uncase
> A soul kept there so sweet, o no.

(From Crashaw's *Carmen Deo Nostro* of 1652, reprinted in *The
Poems: English, Latin, and Greek of Richard Crashaw*, ed. L. C.
Martin [Oxford: Oxford University Press, 1927], pp. 318–19.)
Here also the clothing is a symbol for the body, and nakedness
for the soul.
18. Herodotus *History* I. 8–12.

the problem of the poem is now made evident: this "spouse" could have more than one husband. The bride is a fallen woman, and the character of her fall is revealed equally in the images by which her primal unity has given way to multiplicity and in the multiple lovers to whom she has given herself who are, still, each the husband. The betrayal of the bride by her true lover is an act of grace, a gift from God to fallen men. Unless Christ were willing to reveal his bride in her multiplicity and resulting individuality, how could anyone other than his own specific self ever join her? Or, on the external level, how could the church ever become a historical reality? Yet neither is there any church, nor any marriage between God and man, unless the multiplicity of brides and husbands in some way veils an archetypal bride and husband through whom fundamental unity may be achieved, the figure for which in the poem is John Donne's own person.

While in the first ten lines of the poem the search for the bride seems to be directed chiefly to outside realities, the resolution in the final four lines now takes place by redirecting the search more openly to the (veiled) inner reality. In this inner sanctum, in the holy of holies, the bride's external garb is taken off. How, now, can one express the intense union achieved there? I can express it only by saying nothing or by saying everything at once.

Stripped of her ecclesiastical trappings, who is she but a man, the poet himself, the true bride, the spiritual Israel— and yet not a true bride unless actually joined to her counterpart in the opposite gender, the husband-lover, the Lord, who is also the betrayer, the world itself, the external ecclesia, discoverable also as a man and the poet himself in his full, complete presence as a body and a soul joined. And yet she is still also the external church, the dove, being courted by "myne amorous soul," who steps now into the place of the archetypal Christ and who, being generated from before all ages from the Father, is reborn within individual man as his primal power of generation—"I in Christ and Christ in me," as Saint Paul expresses the paradox. The poet's own spirit is now Christ the husband, and the bride of Christ is his body (and by analogy the whole variety of churches in history). Hence, the inner self once felt as female (as Jung, the Old Testament, and Donne in his earlier poems all had it) now appears as male. When Christ is born into existence, the psychic principle, as well as the divine figure outside the created world, is discovered to be male; hence when the individual psyche is reborn "in Christ," "she" becomes "he," presenting the man in whom it happens with creative potency which penetrates and activates the flesh rather than the other way around.

It is this meaning of the poem, in which Christ as well as the spouse is finally understood to be an aspect of Donne himself—displeasing though it may be to many of my readers, and tenuous as it is—which leads me to consider the traditional dating correct. It shows Donne spiritually mature or, in traditional Christian terms, regenerate. The earlier "love of God" poems showed him unfulfilled; in these poems his own spirit is represented as passive, inadequate, longing, but lost; where its gender is shown, it is a woman. Even at the time of writing the *Anniversaries* (where, nevertheless, I believe the switch was occurring in Donne's life), Donne's spirit was represented in female form, and the figure of the male divinity is exclusively (or seems exclusively to be) represented as otherworldly. But now, in his later years, after being ordained, in the spiritual confidence of his having joined the external church in the most meaningful way for his own life, and possibly also as a result of the death of his natural wife, he is able to discover the man within and the woman without (as well as vice versa).

By the time of this poem, then, Donne's own person has

become inextricable from both "Christ" and the "spouse," and in the light of this union the problem of Donne's churchmanship appears in a new way. By having treated the poem as a sonnet on Christ's spouse rather than on the church, we have been able to see better what it says about the church: that it is true to Christ in its falseness, that it is clothed in its shamelessness, unified in its multiplicity, spiritual in its historicity, personal in its impersonality, female in its maleness—or, in respect to the traditional question raised for Donne's biography, Catholic in its Protestantism. Seen in this light, "Show me, deare Christ" seems to be Donne's final resolution of the problem of national sectarianism. Neither the Anglican church, nor the other national sects, nor the Catholic church, understood now in the rapidly fragmenting world situation as the Roman Catholic church, nor the church fragmented in time by the processes of history (as in lines 5 and 6, which I have not commented on) or by geography (referred to in lines 7 and 8 and elsewhere) is prevented thereby from being also the one true church. The multiple churches and the one church are the same; so is it that, in having joined the fallen bride of Christ, John Donne also joined the true.

There is nothing particularly new about this for Donne's life in a conventional sense; he had said nearly the same thing in correspondence before he was ordained. The new things are the discovery of the figure of Christ in his inner life, the completeness with which the inner life now joins the historical church, and the identity of his own integrated person with the marriage between Christ and his bride. That the psychic reality should appear now in the male person and the bodily in the female reverses the gender in which these appeared in the third Satire and the earlier "love of God" sonnets. No juncture between the inner life and the external world had been represented in the earlier sonnets at all, and in the *Anniversaries* the external world is joined through Elizabeth Drury and the Drury family, not through the historical church; "A Litany" does join private experience to the public form of the litany, but that form is only an aspect of the church; and in the third Satire the ecclesiastical types who appear are all satirized. Satire appears in "Show me deare Christ," of course ("What, is it she . . . ?"), but it is joined to the nonsatiric in the resolution. The poem represents Donne's acknowledgement that in his own life the fallen world of experience joins the unfallen archetypes of the psyche, and he is not afraid to believe that the experience can be expressed in a dominantly holy poem as well as in such a dominantly secular one as, say, "The Canonization"—an admission he was not ready to make at the time of the third Satire. As "The Canonization" asserted that the natural love affair is holy, so "Show me deare Christ" asserts that the holy love affair is natural.

"We cannot help missing the image of the natural man in the poet's image of the spiritual man," says Miss Gardner in deprecating the poetic worth of Donne's religious poetry; [19] it is where the religious and the poetic join most deeply in her introductory remarks, and it is what I objected to most fundamentally when, in Chapter IV (p. 69), I said that I believed her "aesthetic faulty, her Christian knowledge weak." Her remark shows ignorance of natural theology, in which nature is not denied or destroyed by grace but fulfilled by it. And it is factually wrong: the poet's image of the spiritual man is entirely built out of images of the natural man. If we miss the image of the natural man in this poem or in his other religious poems, it is because we have closed our eyes whenever he appears; perhaps that is a natural defense against the radical and shocking way in which he carries out the implications of

19. Gardner, *The Divine Poems,* p. xvi.

the marital image in this poem. But it is shocking only for those for whom the "holy" cannot also include the primitive. What Donne said and did in his lifetime is not as astonishing as Hosea's actions and explanations, but Donne lived in a later period of history, already further from primitive experience and feeling. Yet Donne lived closer to primitive experience than civilized men have generally since his time.

The extraordinary plainness with which the spiritual man is presented in the image of natural man in this particular poem of Donne's is a good enough reason, I think, to explain why this poem survived in only one manuscript. Donne might well have felt about it as he did about *Biathanatos,* which he said he did not want published yet did not want destroyed.[20] Donne must certainly have been close enough to the spirit of the new Puritanism, right at hand in the person of Archbishop Abbot, to have realized the effect the "impurities" of this poem would have had. "Show me deare Christ" was first printed in 1899, about as early in modern history as it could have been received—and perhaps a little earlier.

In my effort in this book to exculpate the "religious" John Donne from charges brought against him by an over-zealous puritanism, I have perhaps been trying to out-puritan the puritans. I am thinking not only of those nineteenth- and twentieth-century "religious" puritans like Gosse for whom Donne's Christianity was too worldly but also of those "nonreligious" neopuritans in the universities for whom his worldliness is too Christian. Theirs is no more a true puritanism than a true Anglicanism; neither group were Manichaeans. Yet we must cope with the fact that in our own time Donne belongs chiefly to the "nonreligious" rather than to the "religious" puritans (except insofar as all

20. In a letter to Sir Robert Ker, Gosse, *Life,* II, 124.

religious groups are also a part of the new secular society);
and it is against this bastion of secular neopuritans that his
"religious" life and poetry must make its way as best it can.
How far will it be able to go? Can the new secular
university actually receive "Show me deare Christ"?

To be sure, contemporary man lives in an era of new,
so-called sexual freedom, and that suggests a certain kind
of receptivity to the imagery in this poem which the old
puritans (presumably) did not have. But this new freedom
—is it merely a bodily freedom? Are we free enough that
we also can participate in the spiritual marriage? Now that
the spouse of Christ has peeped up before our eyes through
Donne's poem, dare we permit her to be disclosed in her
naked, *and betrayed,* form before our very eyes? Or must
we insist that she show herself clothed? To be sure, we
could not have her as Donne did unless she were also
clothed. But are we capable of receiving her either way,
naked in her impure purity or clothed with pure impurity?
Can we see that she and we are the same, simply man, not
John Donne the man only, an objective and separate histor-
ical person like Jesus of Bethlehem, but man the corporate
person in whatever true-and-fallen form she and you and I
may be joined in our own time? We shall not be able to
receive her, I think, unless we are able in literary classes in
secular colleges and universities to recover from the com-
mitment to romantic innocence (and its special forms of
experience) that has become entrenched in English depart-
ments in America. Has the Judaeo-Christian language and
tradition been driven underground or banished because we
are so deeply convinced that the spouse is in fact the whore
of Babylon Miss Gardner thought Donne's was? Certainly
the ecclesia, and the tradition she bears, is fallen, as Israel,
in the figure of Hosea's whore-wife Gomer, was before her;
and to acknowledge her in any wise is to acknowledge
oneself a companion in the same condition. But only if our

fallen condition can be reconciled to the paradisial vision, whether of the past or the future, can we marry our own souls—and become men. If she can be acknowledged—in some way or other—then the fallen bride, peeping out in Donne's poem where she has lain hidden under the veil of several centuries, can image again not merely a sectarian experience but a universal human one. Then she, and Donne, could help to rejoin a world whose threatening fragmentation may otherwise indeed fulfill that other image of the whore.

APPENDIX

This appendix is supplied as indicated in footnote 26 of Chapter IV. The passage from the *Summa Theologica* is quoted from the *Basic Writings of Saint Thomas Aquinas,* the English Dominican translation, chiefly by Fr. Laurence Shapcote, O.P., edited, revised, and corrected by Anton Pegis, 2 vols. (New York: Random House, 1945), II, 488.

Question LXIV
ON THE MEAN OF VIRTUE

. . . .

First Article

WHETHER THE MORAL VIRTUES CONSIST IN A MEAN?

We proceed thus to the First Article:—
Objection 1. It would seem that moral virtue does not consist in a mean. For the nature of a mean is incompatible with that which is extreme. Now the nature of virtue is to be something extreme; for it is stated in *De Caelo* i. that *virtue is the peak of power.* Therefore moral virtue does not consist in a mean.

Obj. 2. Further, the maximum is not a mean. Now some moral virtues tend to a maximum: for instance, magnanimity to very great honors, and magnificence to very large expenditures, as is stated in *Ethics* iv. Therefore not every moral virtue consists in a mean. . . .

On the contrary, The Philosopher says that *moral virtue is an elective habit consisting in the mean.*

I answer that, As has already been explained, the nature of virtue is that it should direct man to good. . . . But the good of that which is measured or ruled consists in its conformity with its rule; and, thus, the good of things made by art is that they follow the rule of art. . . . Hence it is evident that the good of moral virtue consists in conformity with the rule of reason. Now it is clear that between excess and deficiency the mean is equality or conformity. Therefore it is evident that moral virtue consists in a mean.

Reply Obj. 1. Moral virtue derives its goodness from the rule of reason, while its matter consists in passions or operations. If, therefore, we compare moral virtue to reason, then, if we look at that which it has of reason, it holds the position of one extreme, viz., conformity; while excess and defect take the position of the other extreme, viz., deformity. But if we consider moral virtue in respect of its matter, then it has the nature of a mean, in so far as it makes the passion conform to the rule of reason. Hence the Philosopher says that *virtue, as to its essence, is a mean,* in so far as the rule of virtue is imposed on its proper matter; *but it is an extreme in reference to the "best" and "the excellent,"* viz., as to its conformity with reason.

Reply Obj. 2. In actions and passions, the mean and the extremes depend on various circumstances. Hence nothing hinders something from being extreme in a particular virtue according to one circumstance, while the same thing is a mean according to other circumstances, through its conformity with reason. This is the case with magnanimity and magnificence. . . . There will be excess, if one tends to this maximum *when* it is not right, or *where* it is not right, or for an undue *end;* and there will be deficiency if one fails to tend thereto *where* one ought, and *when* one ought. This agrees with the saying of the Philosopher that the *magnanimous man observes the extreme in quantity, but the mean in the right mode of his action.*

INDEX

Abbot, Archbishop, 143
Abelard, 11
Adam, 16; Jesus as the second, 17
Adultery, signifies idolatry, 158
Aesthetic: faulty, 69; model of sexual consummation, 167
Affections: faculty of the soul, 111; forcing the, 71, 72; inordinate, 62, 83; in poem, 110; true, 63
Alice in Wonderland, 20
Alienation: Donne's experience of, 88, 89; of the psyche, 111
Allegory, of Song of Solomon, 160–61
Andrewes, Lancelot, 130
Anglican, 19, 37; Donne as, 19, 37, 58, 78, 80, 81, 91, 94, 95, 124, 128, 143, 148, 149, 151–52, 153; nature of, 148–49, 152–53; political aspects of, 77, 78; visible, 37. *See also* Church, Anglican; Jesuit, Anglicized
Anima mundi, 102, 113
Aquinas, Saint Thomas, 45, 144, 145; Aristotelianism of, 15
Archetype: bride and husband, 172; C. G. Jung's, 8, 115; Christ, 4, 172; of generation, 169; idea of a

woman, 114; marriage, in the Bible, 162; of Old Testament, 161; Platonic, 115; resurrection, 115; unfallen, 175
Aristotelian, 15, 45, 111
Aristotle, 14, 40
Arminian, 153
Augustine, Saint, 40
Augustinian model of time, 7

Bacon, Sir Francis, 18
Balance, 59, 64, 70, 72, 75, 82
Bald, R. C., 26, 120, 121
Bartlett, Lady, 133
Benefice, acceptance of, 57, 61, 83
Bernini, Giovanni Lorenzo, 34
Beza, 90
Bible, 15, 16, 115, 129, 155; Amos, 158; Ezekiel, 158; Hosea, 158, 162, 176, 177; Isaiah, 158; Jeremiah, 158, 159; Lamentations, 163; marital imagery of, 155; Nicodemus' objection to Jesus, 115; Protestant connection with, 16; rediscovery of antiquity, 15; Song of Solomon, 160–61; supports Catholic position, 129. *See also* Scripture
Body: Donne's is bride of Christ, 173; Donne not a part of, 88, 89; image of

consciousness, 109; of Israel, 156; preserved from putrefaction, 116; relationship to psyche, 100; of world, 88, 149
Botticelli, 18
Bride: community of the church, 162; of God, not whore of Babylon, 162; seen only when naked, 170; speaker is the, 169. *See also* Christ, spouse of; Nakedness; Marriage
Brooke, Christopher, 120
Broughton, Hugh, 81
Browne, Sir Thomas, 151, 152
The Burial of Count Orgaz (El Greco), 43, 46
Bush, Douglas, 81, 146

Calvinist, 61, 62, 152
Candaules, King, 171
Canterbury, 150
Casuist, 60, 65, 79
Catholic, 34, 35, 37, 61, 129, 174. *See also* Church, Catholic; Church, Roman Catholic
Catholicism, 37, 41, 152
Catholics, 41, 58, 148; English, 78; medieval, 36
Certainty of salvation, 152
Charles, Prince of Wales, 142
Charles II, King, 19
"Cherry Tree Carol," 15
Chillingworth, William, author of *The Religion of Protestants a Safe Way to Salvation,* 152
Christ: body of, 13; body of, is male, 162; bride of, is female, 162; the divine husband, in Bible, 162; historical event in, 109; identity of, 169; image of the divine immanence, 168; psyche able to copy his action, 103; spouse of, 154; wash in blood of, 108

Christendom: forms of, 95; hierarchies of medieval, 13; wickedness of, 91; willingness to die for, 95
Christian: ambivalence, 75; Aristotelianism, 15; attitudes, 74; choice of death, 92; community, 161; despising of the world, 72; Donne's attitude basically, 72; Donne's view of, 93, 141; of Donne's world experience, 77; experience tepid, 68; history basis of psychic marriage, 103; humanism, 99; knowledge, 69, 175; person, 73; polarity of, 45; reproduction, 103; symbols, 168; test of faith, 94; tradition, 9, 72, 93; traditional terms, 173; worldliness, 12, 75, 176
Christianity, 9, 25, 72, 74, 149; comparison to sun, 150; Donne's, 9, 176; French Catholic form of, 129; world-negation in, 74
Christology, development of Logos, 168
Church: antiseptic term, 154; as it appears in the world, 147; as best of existing churches, 147; Catholic, 35, 147 (*see also* Catholic; Roman Catholic); Donne's relation to, 18, 29, 46, 82, 122, 123, 124, 125, 141, 174 (*see also* Churchmanship); English Roman Catholic, 37, 91; external, 166; fragmented, 174; headed by king, 78; the historical, 48, 174; invisible, 29, 39, 122; joining of external and internal, 172; a male and female identity, 162; a man, the little world of, 169; medieval English, 37; one

true, 174; primitive, 86; promised in Scripture, 147 (*see also* Christ, bride of; Christ, spouse of; Christ, body of); reformed, 66; resolution of conflict about, 46; Roman, 47, 81, 132; Roman Catholic, 37, 66, 78, 81, 82, 91, 126, 174 (*see also* Catholic; Roman Catholic; Christendom); in "Show me deare Christ," 174; sonnet on, 148; sonnet, not about the, 153; state, 78; true, reconciled to fallen, 165; visible, 28, 29, 32, 36, 37, 38, 48, 66 (*see also* Anglican, visible); visible and invisible, 35, 148; visible, joined to Christ, 166

Church, Anglican, 4, 19, 48, 54, 81, 82, 146, 152, 174; when Donne joined, 18. *See also* Anglican; *Via media*

Church of England, 56, 127; images of, 48; loyalty to, 146

Churchmanship: problem of Donne's, 148, 174; summary of stages in Donne's, 82, 143

Communion, as mental discipline, 41

Conscience: actual, 65; Donne's problem of, 60; instructed, 60, 65; invisible, 60; violation of Donne's, 59, 82

Consciousness: as God, 105; as manipulator, 106. *See also* Reason; Unconscious

Conversion: Donne's, to Anglicanism, 48; Gosse's view of Donne's, 136; plural in Donne, says Gosse, 50

Cope, Sir Walter, 127, 128

Counter Reformation, 39, 40

Court: difficulty of achieving preferment from, 78; Donne absent from, 86, 140; Donne closer to, through Drury, 127; Donne to give up, 57, 58; epithalamium not meant to flatter, 139; not exclusive of church interests, 128; symbol of the old way, 97; symbolized the world, 67, 74, 77, 124, 141

Covenant, in the Old Testament, 156

Creation, 159

Critical: aspect of this book, 6, 7; tradition in scholarship dangerous, 153

Critiques (Kant's), 153

Cupid, 138

Dante, 12, 45

David (Old Testament), 157, 160

Death: definition of, 87; Donne's longing for, 92; Donne's preoccupation with, 85; in Donne's writing, 84; of Elizabeth Drury, 113, 117; of Sir Robert Drury, 121; dying to this world, 72; "enfranchised thee," 117; feeling of, 100; freedom of soul in, 117; function of, 87; great issues of, 4; images of, 97; imaginative, 118; metaphorical, 86, 89, 116; physical, 118; at the point of, 84; problem of, 20; psychic, 87; rightly chosen, 92; senses of, in Donne's writing, 20, 84, 86, 87, 89, 115, 116, 118, 138; this body of, 116; wish of John Donne, 85, 95; wish, rejected, 96

Despair, 32, 72, 101, 104

Devil: under control of, 112; tempts us to choose a good thing, 92

Distortion: in Donne's "Litanie," 67; halting, lurching, leaping, 54; in inner and outer life, 50; in reconciliation of inner and outer, 42

Divine Comedy, 15

Divinity, a formal body of knowledge, Donne's relationship to, 47, 123, 126

Doncaster, Lord Hay, 126

Donne and the Drurys (R. C. Bald), 120

"Do Not Go Gentle into That Good Night" (Dylan Thomas), 21

Doubt, 33, 152. *See also* Skepticism

Drury, Elizabeth, 113, 115, 120, 122, 175

Drury family, Donne's relationship to, 120, 121

Drury, Sir Robert, 120, 122, 123, 124, 127, 132, 140; R. D., 140

Duality: affirmation and negation, 89; Aristotle and Bible, 41; art and nature, 14; biography and literary analysis, 54; body-psyche, 100, 105; body and soul, 14, 99, 172; body and soul, debate between, 31; Catholic and Protestant, 19, 50; Cavalier and Puritan, 14; choosing and not choosing, 89; of the church, 172; in churches joined, 174; church and state, 14, 126; conscious and unconscious, 104, 106; death and birth, 118; death and life, 89; death and rebirth, 112; depression and excitement, 85; devil-God, 100; Donne and ourselves, 177; doubt and confidence, 151; dual-

ism, not same as, 17; external and internal, 54, 59, 96; external and temporal, 118; financial and spiritual, 58; flesh and soul, 30, 44; foolishly and prudently, 78; forcing the opposite, 63; God and man, 13, 14, 118; God's love and Satan's hate, 105; good and evil, 70; growth of a sense of, 10; health and sickness, 63, 71; heaven and earth, 118; honor and dishonor, 63, 71; inner and outer, 43, 44, 46, 59, 74, 83, 89, 119; intellect and emotion, 14, 44, 48; interior and exterior, 67; Jack Donne and John Donne, 49; joined, 21, 50, 172, 173; law and grace, 108; less well-known variants, 15; love and death, 84; male-female, 103, 112, 162; man's will and God's will, 62; mannerist, 46, 53; medieval and modern, 50; in the metaphysical style, 53; might or might not, 139; mystical and active life, 144; new, 45; Old and New Testaments, 41; the one and the many, 14; pairs of alternatives, 150; past and present, 10, 15; personal, 28; poetry and religion, 50; political and ecclesiastical, 96; poverty and riches, 70; private to public, 119; psyche and soma, 54; reason and emotion, 50, 52; reason and faith, 45; religious or secular, 21; religious and worldly, 69; resolved by Anglicanism, 152; Rome and Geneva, 152; sacred and secular, 14, 45, 96; secular and religious, 175;

self and other-than-self, 76; short or long life, 63; sin and salvation, 14; skepticism and faith, 151; speaker and auditor, 30; specific image and the self-reflective power, 32; spiritual and ecclesiastical, 96; spiritual-material, 103; spiritual and practical, 25; spiritual and temporal, 78; temporal and external, 118; this life and the next, 13; this world and the other, 13, 72, 76, 96, 100, 118; thought and prayer, 45; tradition of great cleavages, 50; two persons of one self, 30; two separate sacred Donnes, 50; two things, opposite, 34; two worlds, 21; upper and lower, 44; visible and invisible, 29, 30, 35; vocational and religious, 25; wealth and poverty, 63, 71; well-known variants, 14; will and reason, 104; world and spirit, 73. *See also* Balance; Marriage; Polarity; Reconciliation; Reformation-Renaissance

Dunn, Sir Daniell, 130, 137

Egerton, Sir Thomas, 23, 81, 86
El Greco, *The Burial of Count Orgaz,* 43, 46; *Laocoön,* 44
Eliot, T. S., 68, 88
Elizabeth, Princess, 140
Elizabeth, Queen, 36
Elizabethans, characteristics of, 10
Emotion, 52, 53, 93; in religion and poetry, 49
Empson, William, 114
Essex, Earl of, 132
Existential, 53; existence, 5, 51, 85, 89, 173

Female, 157, 160; feminine, 101, 115; Israel, 157, 159, 162; persona, 102, 111
Fideism, Donne's religion a form of, 151
Figure: of Christ, 168, 174; of Donne's own person, 172; female, 157; Logos, 169; male, 159, 173; of the spouse, 154, 155; of spouse in Bible, 163–64; of whore in Bible, 162
Figures: of New Testament among Catholics, 41; of Old Testament among Puritans, 41
Flesh, 31, 72, 73, 100, 101, 102, 110

"G. B.," 133, 135
"G. K." (same as "G. B."), 132, 133, 136
Gardner, Helen, 40, 47, 60, 70, 72, 177; criticism of, 52, 67–69, 72, 162, 175–76; dating of Divine Poems, 27, 50, 61, 104; dating of "A Litanie," 81; her interpretation of "A Litanie," 67–70, 75; her interpretation of "Show me deare Christ," 146–48, 154–55, 162, 163
Gerrard, Mr., 133, 134, 136
Goodyer, Sir, Henry, 66, 80, 87, 88, 92, 128
Gosse, Edmund, 27, 36, 81, 87, 124, 126, 130, 131, 132, 133, 136, 142; criticism of, 48–50, 52, 66, 85, 120–21, 125, 130, 131–33, 136, 140–41, 142; *Life and Letters of John Donne,* 26, 48, 134
Grace, 108, 110, 175
The Great Exemplar (Jeremy Taylor), 3
Greseley, Sir G., 133

Grierson, Herbert J. C., 131, 146

Hadas, Moses, 93
Hammarskjöld, Dag, 144, 145
Hay, Lord (Doncaster), 124, 126
Herodotus, 171
Hesiod, 115
Heywood, Henry, 37
Heywood, Jasper, 36, 37
Homer, 115
Hope, 32
Hopkins, Gerard Manley, 16
Howard, Lady, 130, 134

Image: bride, 165, 178; Christ, 169; churches as persons, 32; "gellie," 139; historical church, 48; Israel, 159; Jerusalem, 155, 163; light in Plato, 14, 17; light or vegetation, 168; man, 32, 175; marriage, 97; movement of soul, mirror of, 43; personal and fleshly, 112; poem (of virtue), 118; poet, 30, 175; sexual and marital, 97, 98, 170, 176; spouse, 155; "Sunne" and "Son," 20; town, 112; whore, 178
Incarnation, 72, 110
Indifference, 64, 70, 82, 92; definition of, 63, 64; important state of, 62, 63; purpose of, 64, 65
Ingram, Sir Ar., 133
Initiative: God to take, 105, 107, 112, 118; lack of, 107; man's, 107, 108, 118; masculine, 101
Inner life: categories of, 44; conflict in, 58, 60, 82; dangers of, 75; deep cultivation of, 41; Donne a hero of, 72; dual, 45; language as joining, 54; linked to world, 54, 88,

120; the mannerist, 44, 51; models of, 45, 97; the new, 39, 40, 84; as religious, 41, 70, 154; separate from outer life, 41, 42
Israel: figure of, 177; the interior, 158–66, 172; the true, 162; why gender of switches, 159

Jansenism, 153
James, King, 56, 123, 126, 140, 143
Jesuit(s): detached inner life, 39–41; Donne an Anglicized, 144; Donne's relationship to, 95, 96; new style of relationship of authority, 78; refuse allegiance to king, 91; secret priest, 36
Jesuitical Catholicism, 96, 144
Johnson, Samuel, 54
Jonson, Ben, 119, 131
Jung, C. G., 8; animus and anima, 159
Jungian idea of a woman, 114

Kant, author of: *Critiques*, 153; *Religion within the Limits of Reason Alone*, 153
Ker, Sir Robert, 131
King: access to, 138; authority of, 129; direct service to, 144; of England, 129; French, 129; obedience to, 77; political and religious symbol, 78; as political symbol, 74, 77; service to, not merely secular, 126
King-husband, power of the spiritual, 102
King, Dr. John, 79; bishop of London, 143

Lamentations, spouse as she appears in, 169
Laocoön (El Greco), 44

Latin definition of virtue,
114
Law, Donne's interest in, 126
Lewis, C. S., 21
Life, great issues of, 4
"Life of Dr. John Donne"
(Izaak Walton), 28
*Life and Letters of John
Donne* (Edmund Gosse),
26, 48, 134
Limburg brothers, paintings of,
12
Lincoln's Inn, 121, 143;
benchers of, 126
Lipsius, Justus, 14
Literary method of this
book, 6
Logos, 169
Lord: death for the sake of,
92; transfiguration of, 162
Lord's faithfulness, living
parable of, 158
Love: actual movement of,
109; affair between God
and man, 112; in Donne's
writing, 84; of God, 84,
104, 105, 110; rises up in
man's breast, 110; of
speaker, 111
Lover from the other world,
101
Loyola, Saint Ignatius of:
author of *Spiritual Ex-
ercises,* 4, 40, 60, 61, 62,
63; tradition of, 60, 64
Lukewarmness, characteristic
of Christians, 69

Madonna with the Long Neck
(Parmigianino), 44
Male: interchanged with
female, 159, 174; Israel,
157, 159; Lord in Hebrew-
Christian tradition, 99;
persona, 102; psyche, 173
Manley, Frank, 27, 114
Mannerism: definition of, 6,
44, 51; disjunction in, 43,
46, 104; in Donne's life
and writing, 54, 68, 119,

141, 145, 149; in painting,
6, 43; in religion, 75, 118,
144, 149; Shearman's
book on, 6; in the story of
the psychic marriage, 99;
style of, 6, 34, 43, 44, 46,
50, 51, 54, 58, 76, 77, 87;
the term, its values and
limitations for this study,
6, 8, 51; in virtue, 76, 77,
78; a way of life, 43, 44,
54, 58, 76, 77, 78, 87.
See also Distortion
Marriage: archetype in Bible,
155, 162; of Christ and
his spouse, 166, 172, 174;
consummation of, 101, 161,
165; Donne's, 22, 25, 112,
122, 145; Donne's attitude
toward Rochester's, 137,
141; in Herodotus' story,
171; of Lady Howard to
Rochester, 130; of man to
God, 100, 107, 112, 118,
119, 122, 162, 165, 172,
174; metaphorical, 97, 118,
167, 169; psychic (chapter
on), 98–123; psychic, as
inner union, 166; psychic,
meaning of, for Donne,
171 f.; as rape, 111; spirit-
ual, 177
Martz, Louis: author of
Poetry of Meditation, 3, 27,
40, 47, 52, 60; criticism
of, 52; explanation of
prayer, 47
Mary, Virgin, 119, 120
Mass, 35, 39, 41
Medieval (Middle Ages):
Anglican church a survi-
val of the, 144; Christen-
dom, 37, 38, 41, 42, 75;
Donne's relationship to the,
18, 96, 144; phenomenon
of the, 11, 16; style, 12,
15, 18, 42, 45, 79
Meditation: Catholic and
Protestant, 41; form of
mediation, 118

Meditative: an interpretative term for Donne's poetry, 52, 53; traditional marks in "Show me deare Christ," 147, 168

Merrill, Charles Edmund, Jr., 132

Metaphor: bride, 156, 172; children of Israel is not, 156; complexities of, 167; death, 86; Elizabeth Drury ("she"), 115, 119; geographical, 148; hill-of-truth, 33; inappropriate, 119; inner life for outer world, 168; ladder in medieval period, 12; marital, 111, 118, 160, 162, 167, 169, 176; nakedness for the soul, 171; sexual, 111; soul, 113; sun, 149; "Sunne" and "Son," 20. *See also* Archetypes; Figure; Image

Metaphysical style: connection of, to Scholastic logic, 18; definition of, 51–53; relationship of, to "mannerism" and "meditative," 51–53

Moore, Ann (Ann Donne), 22, 23

Morbidity, Donne's, 86, 94

More, Sir George, 23, 25

Morton, Thomas (Dean of Gloucester): conceived hope of ministry for Donne, before King James?, 143; exchange of correspondence with Donne in 1612, 125, 126; story of his offer of preferment to Donne in 1609, 56–82, 89, 124

Myth: of androgynous man, 115; definition of, 97; of divine marriage, 109, 110

Nakedness, 169, 171

New Testament, 17, 40, 72; bride of God does not appear as a whore in, 162; consummation of psychic marriage in, 161, 162; not merely a description of facts, 161; spouse of God originated in Old Testament, 156; whore of Babylon in, 162

Nicene Creed, formulations made conventional in, 169

Oath of Obedience, 56, 81

Old Testament: archetypes of, renewed in New Testament, 161; spouse of New Testament had its origin in (story of the bride-whore Israel), 156–64

On the Soul (Aristotle), 40

On the Trinity (Saint Augustine), 40

Ordination, Donne's, 19, 58, 127, 143, 147

Otherworldly: definition of, 71; Donne never merely, 70, 72, 145; male divinity as, 173. *See also* World, other

Paman, Clement, 121

Paradox, 10, 18, 173

Parmigianino, painter of *Madonna with the Long Neck,* 44

Paul, Saint, 73, 87, 102, 116, 173

Persona: definition of, 98; demonic, 106; of the devil, 105, 106, 107; reversal of, 102, 103

Phenomenology, 6, 9, 51

Phillips, J. B., 73

Plato, 8, 14, 15, 115, 116

Platonic: idea of a woman, 114; insight, accession of, 14; myth of androgynous man, 114

Platonism: challenge to Aristotelianism, 45; new in world of learning, 13
Poetry of Meditation (Louis Martz), 3
Polarity, 14, 18, 19, 27, 79; doubt and faith, 19; north and south, 149; problem of, in this book, 54; relationship of, to mannerism, 6. *See also* Duality
Pope: adherence to test of Christian faith, 94, 96; authority of, 78, 129; the one hierarch, 40
Prayer: as access to subconscious, 64; in "A Litanie," 72; meaning of, 47; mental, 41, 53, 67; as term for "emotion," 45; vocational purpose of, 60; whole point of, 64
Protestant: characteristic of, 15, 17, 39; in Donne's later life, 174; question of visibility, 34, 35, 41. *See also* Duality, Catholic and Protestant
Psyche: biblical categories of, 41, 44; conscious and unconscious aspects of, 103; image of the divine immanence, 168; interchangeable with "soul," 40; joined to body, 13, 77, 100, 102, 106; personified, 99, 100, 102, 103, 107, 111, 173; place of aesthetic experience, 43; place of unfallen world, 175; regenerated, 73, 103; sexual transformation of, 102; three faculties of (as memory, reason, and/or will), 40, 41, 44, 45, 47, 48, 49, 50, 53, 59, 90
Psychology, 6, 66; depth, 51; same as "spiritual life," 97
Psychotherapist, a "spiritual director," 60

Purgatorio (Dante), 12
Puritan: Donne as anti-, 97; worldliness of, 74, 96

Quakers, 13, 18

Ramism, 13
Ramus, Peter, 14
Reconciliation: in Donne's life, 50; of dualities, 118; of extremes, 76; of the fallen churches to the one true church, 165; in the growing polarities, 54; hidden, 75; human communication, 42; implied in "mannerism," 51; in the inner life, 42; of the male and female, 166; of man to God, 32; of multiplicity with unity, 165; of ourselves with Donne's values, 178; represented by poem, 118; in this book, 54; of the true and false bride, 165; twisted, 67; of world polarities, 77
Redemption, 72
Reformation-Renaissance: distinguished from medieval, 11 f.; mode of apprehension, 15; polarities not new in, 14; style of, 18, 19; uneasy about church, 13
Regeneration: by "Christ," 169; in man's psyche, 73, 103; 173
Religion. *See* Anglican; Catholic; Christian; Church; Protestant; Religious
Religious: Donne's position, 25, 29, 50, 69, 82, 145, 176; language 9; life, 28, 66; poetry, 68, 98; secular neopuritans, 177
Renaissance, 12, 18, 79
Renaissance-Reformation, 45, 99; Janus-headed term, definition of, 9, 10

Resolution: in Donne's life, 59, 82, 143, 145; of inner and outer, 58, 141; in painting, 43–44, 46; by paradox, 152; in poem, 108, 109, 167, 168, 170

Revised Standard Version, 73

Richer, Edmond, 128–29

Roberts, Donald Ramsay, author of "The Death Wish of John Donne," 85, 95, 96

Robinson, H. Wheeler, 156

Rochester, Earl of Somerset, 123, 124, 130, 131, 134, 137, 140

Roman Catholic: absence from Anglican church services, 35; Donne brought up as, 77, 143. *See also* Catholic; Church, Catholic; Church, Roman Catholic

Roman Catholicism: definition of, 77, 96, 128; in England, 37, 95, 96, 130; Gallican wing of, 130, 153; not wicked to Donne, 91

Saint Peter's Cathedral, mannerism in, 34

Salvation: in Calvinism, 62; certainty of, 151, 152; doubt of, 151, 152

Satire, of external church, 32, 175

Scholastic, 13, 45; identification of logos, 114; language, 18; logic, 18; methods, 7

Scripture, 147, 154; private interpretation of, 39

Scriptures, systems of interpreting, 12

Seneca, 93

Senecan Stoicism, 93

Sexual: consummation imitated in poem, 167; freedom in our time, 177; transformation, 102; union, 101

Shearman, John, author of *Mannerism*, 6

Simile, in Song of Solomon, 161

Simpson, Evelyn, 36, 80, 90, 146, 148

Skepticism: Donne's 32, 38; the modern term, 29, 46

Song of Solomon. *See* Bible

Soul: brought to justice, 107, 108; equivalent to psyche, 40; king's spoken words entered, 143; memory an aspect of, 48; persona of, 108, 111, 113; relationship to body, 87, 104, 119, 178; relationship to speaker, 107, 110, 178; third faculty of, 47

Spiritual director: a casuist, 60; who was Donne's?, 79

Spiritual Exercises (St. Ignatius of Loyola), 4, 40, 41, 44, 53, 60, 61, 62, 63, 65, 70, 71, 82; Calvinized version of, 4; election in, 62

Spouse: in Bible, 154, 155, 163; of Christ, 154, 165, 177; naked, 177; sonnet on Christ's, 154; true, 169; uncertain identity of, 150

Stationer's Register, 89

Stoicism: in Donne, 72, 93; nature of Senecan, 73, 74, 93

Subconscious, 64

Suicide: in *Biathanatos,* 90; Christian, 93; not martyrdom, 91; proper possibility of, 94, 95; Stoic, 93

Summa: logic of, 13; substance of, 45

Symbol: Christian, 109, 168; of inner life, 74; of the world, court as, 74, 77

Symposium (Plato), 115

Taylor, Jeremy, author of *The Great Exemplar,* 3

Theology, 47, 66, 90

Thisworldly. *See* World, this

Thomas, Dylan, author of "Do Not Go Gentle into That Good Night," 21
Toleration Act of 1689, 19
Trinity, second person of, 114

Uncertainty: about Anglican church, 152; in "Show me, deare Christ," 150
Unconscious, 103, 109, 110; as devil, 105, 106, 107; Donne's death wish is, 95; relationship to consciousness, 106

Via media (middle way): between extremes, 148; includes extremes, 148; man of the, 152
Visible: Christianity is, 34, 35, 37; hierarchical rapprochement, 46; intermediaries, 34
Vocation: absence of, is death, 86, 88; to the church, genuine?, 124, 141; Donne's, 4, 19, 25, 57, 78, 86, 88, 124, 141, 145, 148; law not merely secular, 126; mannerist mode of Donne's, 145; in the *Spiritual Exercises*, 60, 61, 83

Walton, Izaak, 22, 28, 48, 49, 57, 58, 59, 65, 66, 77, 79, 121, 142
Westmoreland Manuscript, 147
Whore: of Babylon, 162, 177; Israel, 155, 162, 177
Wiley, Margaret L., 30
Will: from a hidden source is God's, 64; man's and God's, 61, 62; paralysis of, 89; to

be used in choosing vocation, 61; to be used of goods only, 70
Winchester, Morton, dean of, 125
Wölfflin, Heinrich, author of, *Principles of Art History*, 12
World: affirmation, 74; body of, 88, 149; definition of, 41; despising of, 57, 69, 70, 72, 92; Donne separate from, 76, 86; external, 31, 85, 109, 122, 168; force affections toward, 71; fortune in, 124; good, 70; joining, 87, 89, 122, 143, 145, 178; man not to be conformed to, 73; new (or made new), 17, 73, 74, 77; old, 74; one (whole), 4, 27, 69, 72; other, 4, 11, 20, 67, 71, 76, 104; phenomenon, 41; psyche (life) of, 100, 115, 117; redemption of, 72; symbolized in the court, 67; this, 11, 71, 73, 74, 76, 77, 87, 92, 118
Worldliness: Christian, 74, 75; in death, 91; Donne's, 67, 69, 74; Donne's, estimate of, 143; Donne's, summary of, 145; joined to otherworldliness, 88; in "A Litanie," 75; modernity's definition of, 145. *See also* World
Wotton, Sir Henry, 86, 127

York House, 24

Zion, 155, 157, 163

INDEX TO DONNE'S WORKS

Prose

Biathanatos, 81, 89, 90, 93, 176
Devotions, 3, 4, 142
Essays in Divinity, 116
Ignatius his Conclave, 80, 89
Letters of 1651, 136
Pseudo-Martyr, 28, 46, 48, 49, 50, 78, 80, 81, 82, 89, 91, 93, 96, 126, 129

Poetry

Anniversaries, 112, 114, 118, 119, 120, 173, 174; First Anniversarie, 113, 116, 118, 119; Second Anniversarie, 112, 113, 117–18
The Canonization, 101, 167, 175
To Christ, 19
Divine Meditations, 104, 105, 111, 112, 118, 147, 148
The Divine Poems, 27, 49, 50, 68
Epithalamion: for Princess Elizabeth's wedding, 140; for Rochester and Lady Howard's wedding, 137 f.; Ecclogue, 137–38; Donne's writing of, 130 f.
Holy Sonnets, 61, 67, 68; "As due my many titles I resigne," 104; "Batter my heart, three person'd God," 111; "Father, part of his double interest" (sonnet twelve), 108; "Oh my blacke Soule! now thou art summoned," 107; "Wilt thou love God, as he thee!," 109
A Hymne to God the Father, 19
A Litanie, 66–72, 75–76, 81, 175
Show me deare Christ, 8, 99, 146 ff. (entire chapter); quotations from, 150, 165, 170, 171; Sonnet on Christ's spouse, properly called, 154
Third Satire: discussion of, 29–34, 44, 46, 78, 81, 82, 153, 174, 175
A Valediction: of Weeping, 20, 167